GARY LINEKER

STRIKINGLY DIFFERENT

GARY LINEKER
STRIKINGLY DIFFERENT

A Biography

Foreword by Bobby Charlton

Colin Malam

STANLEY PAUL
LONDON

Stanley Paul & Co Ltd
An imprint of Random House (UK) Ltd
20 Vauxhall Bridge Road, London SW1V 2SA

Random House Australia Pty Ltd
20 Alfred Street, Milsons Point, Sydney, NSW 2061

Random House New Zealand Limited
18 Poland Road, PO Box 40–086, Glenfield, Auckland 10

Random House South Africa Pty Ltd
PO Box 337, Bergvlei 2012, South Africa

First published 1993

Set in Linotronic Sabon by
SX Composing Ltd, Rayleigh, Essex

Printed and bound in Great Britain by
Mackays of Chatham

A catalogue record for this book is available upon
request from the British Library

ISBN 0 09 175424 0

Photographic Acknowledgments

Leicester City portrait, Allsport; Leicester v Spurs, Colorsport; First League goal for
Everton, Colorsport; 1986 FA Cup Final, Allsport; England v Poland 1986, Allsport;
Lineker and Beardsley, Colorsport; England v Spain 1987, Allsport; On the beach,
Colorsport; Steve Archibald, Allsport; European Cup-Winners' Cup 1989, Colorsport;
Johan Cruyff, Allsport; Terry Venables and Irving Scholar, Allsport; First goal FA Cup
Semi-final 1991, Colorsport; Lineker and Gascoigne, Allsport; Lineker with FA Cup,
Allsport; England v West Germany 1990, Colorsport; England training, Colorsport;
European Championship 1992, before Sweden game, Colorsport; England v Poland,
1991, Allsport; England v Sweden, European Championship 1992, substitution, Allsport;
England v France, European Championship 1992, Colorsport; Lineker with young
Japanese fans, Bob Thomas; Training with Grampus Eight, Bob Thomas.

Contents

For my father

FOREWORD

Bobby Charlton

While I would rate Gary Lineker among the greatest finishers football has ever seen, I think he will be remembered more for his marvellous image than for his great skill at putting the ball in the net. His attitude on the field and his demeanour off it really have been something special. He's never been booked or sent off, he's never argued with referees and he's always been very approachable. So I think, in that respect, people will hold him in very high regard.

But he is a very, very skilful player, too. Like Denis Law, Jimmy Greaves and Ferenc Puskas, he is one of the truly gifted finishers: one of the people who just seem to find themselves in goalscoring positions and you wonder how they did it. There is no secret – it was their skill that got them there. Something else that set them apart was that, when confronted by the goalkeeper, they very rarely failed to score. And Gary Lineker comes into that category.

I would put him among the all-time great goalscorers. His record speaks for itself, and it didn't fade towards the end of his career in England, either. His scoring record at Tottenham, in his last season there proved that. When it might have been expected to tail off, it didn't – anything but. He will always score goals in any team, whichever way you play, because balls are going to rebound from the bar, off the post and off the goalkeeper, and he'll be there to pop them in.

In the latter part of his career, he just liked staying up there. If everyone else could get the ball into the box, he'd tidy it up. In that respect, he reminds me strongly of Gerd Müller, the striker who came into the West German team towards the end of my international career. He wasn't interested in anything outside the box, either, though he was probably better in the air than Gary.

It was different in Gary's early days, of course. When he was with Leicester and Everton, he was particularly fast. When he left a defender behind there was no catching him because he was so quick. In fact, I remember him best when he was at Everton and scoring goals through sheer pace.

To be honest, I expected Gary to break my England scoring record for about seven years. He was a young player who was an out-and-out goalscorer, and I thought he would play enough matches to do it. I was surprised, then, when he didn't quite manage it. I wouldn't have minded if he had succeeded, because I couldn't have thought of anyone better to do it, but I have to admit I was quite pleased he didn't.

For a long time, I never really bothered about the record. In fact, I had to think hard to remember when I did what Gary was trying to do. It was against Wales in Cardiff in 1963, I think, that I broke Nat Lofthouse's record of 30 goals for England. But in those days, there was no screaming in the newspapers, and I never really gave it much thought. Norma, my wife, didn't even know I was the record-holder until it started getting mentioned because of Gary. But when he didn't do it, I felt really good because I realised it was a very satisfying record to have. It's there for ever – or at least until another exceptional goalscorer like Gary Lineker comes along.

Introduction

Gary Lineker is, quite simply, the most universally famous and popular footballer England has produced since Bobby Charlton. The boyish, unassuming striker from Leicester may have fallen just short of both Charlton's international goalscoring record and his godlike status, but there can be few places in the world where Lineker would not now be recognised instantly and fêted accordingly. Considering there is no real comparison between the natural gifts of the two players, this is an achievement of some magnitude.

It was all done so quickly, too. A prime example of modern professional football's capacity to transform quite suddenly the lives of its practitioners, Lineker became rich and famous with a speed that might make even Hollywood catch its breath. While not exactly a story of overnight success, his career changed so dramatically for the better in such a short space of time that he could have been forgiven for letting it all go to his head.

One minute, it seemed, Lineker was nothing more than a promising striker with unfashionable Leicester City in what, pre-Premier League, used to be the English First Division: the next, he had scored more goals than anyone else in the finals of the 1986 World Cup and was earning a fortune playing for Barcelona. The year between the summers of 1985 and 1986 represented a time of startlingly rapid progress.

Happily, no allowances have had to be made for the effect on Lineker's ego of the speed of it all. One of the keys – perhaps *the* key – to his enormous popularity at home and abroad has been his ability to take success comfortably in his stride and not let it diminish his natural modesty, politeness and affability. In that sense, he is something of a throwback to turn-of-the-century public school heroism: a resonant echo of lofty Corinthian ideals.

1

As such, Lineker is an ad-man's dream. During a 14-year career he has not once been booked or sent off, while scoring goals like a machine – and being kicked, elbowed and pushed by defenders. He also actually looks and acts the part. Born with a winning smile and darkly handsome still, he steers well clear of priggishness by applying a sharp intelligence and a wry, self-deprecating sense of humour to most of the situations in which he finds himself. Here is a man in unusually firm control of himself and his destiny.

In that sense alone, Lineker is the very antithesis of his former Tottenham and England team-mate, Paul Gascoigne. While Gascoigne, that immensely gifted force of nature, hurtles through life thrilling and appalling by turns, Lineker knows exactly what he is doing and where he is going. His career has been planned as meticulously as the slick penalty-area manoeuvres that brought him 48 goals for England and hundreds more for Leicester, Everton, Barcelona and Tottenham. Only twice, under Johan Cruyff at Barcelona and under Graham Taylor with England, has a spanner been thrown in the smooth-running works.

Undeniably, Lineker is a 'manufactured' footballer. Not blessed with dazzling footwork, a devastating body-swerve or the ability to rip open a defence with one pass, he has worked extremely hard to make the very most of his explosive acceleration, natural athleticism, good balance, perfect timing and priceless ability to find the net from almost any angle within the penalty area. Those who argue that goalscoring is nothing but a matter of instinct are liable to get rather short shrift from this particular master of the craft, this supreme specialist.

While such chastisement would be administered in the nicest possible way, of course, Lineker should not be regarded in any sense as a soft touch. His career is a monument to the steely determination, the dedication, the physical and moral courage required to reach, and stay at, the highest levels of modern sport. Men and women capable of such sustained pursuit of their ambitions are not to be underestimated. In Lineker's case, certainly, the gentle, friendly demeanour and good manners ought never to be mistaken for weakness.

Any doubts about his strength of character cannot have survived his exemplary handling of the shattering news that his first child, George, had developed leukaemia when less than two months old. Lineker is not the only footballer to have found himself in this sort of nightmarish situation – Kim Vilfort, the Danish international midfielder, and Bryan Gunn, Norwich's Scottish international goal-keeper, are others whose children have fallen victim to the disease – but he is probably the one with the highest profile to have done so. Though obviously poleaxed by the blow initially, he resumed playing and scoring for Tottenham and England with admirable speed and resilience.

However, the trauma – and the threat to George's life – was severe enough to discourage Gary from going ahead with a pro-jected autobiography. For the same reason, he also declined to be interviewed directly for what might be called an 'authorised' biography. What he and his agent, Jon Holmes, did agree to do was give me full permission to speak to anyone, pro or con, for the pur-poses of this biography. Indeed, Jon went out of his way on several occasions to help me contact interviewees, and his support for the whole project was unfailing. That said, I hope the chapters which follow will indicate that a real effort has been made to make this assessment of Lineker as objective as possible. It would be incorrect to call it a 'warts and all' picture of England's most famous goal-scorer, since you would struggle to find anything resembling a pimple, never mind a wart, on his polished career. But where criti-cism of the player has been found, it has been given voice.

Most of it comes in the chapter on Lineker's two years as captain of England under the management of Graham Taylor, which culmi-nated in the controversy of his substitution in his last match for his country, a crucial European Championship game in Sweden.

Originally, Lineker had decided not to be interviewed for this biography, either. However, when Jon Holmes made him aware of what Taylor had said about their two years together, he was so in-censed that he insisted on the right of reply. 'I just wanted to give my side of the story,' he said, 'especially in a book about me.'

This book had to be written in such a short time that it could not have been completed on schedule, or thereabouts, without the help, support and encouragement of many people, including the journal-ists and writers Graham Turner, Jack Rollin, Rob Hughes, Jeff Powell, Lynton Guest, Patrick Barclay, Alex Montgomery and David Welch, the sports editor of the *Daily* and *Sunday Telegraph*, and my colleagues in the sports departments of those newspapers.

Roddy Bloomfield, publishing director of Stanley Paul, my wife, Jacqui, and my sons, Paul, Jamie, Jody and Joshua, were other rocks to which I clung from time to time. Thanks are due, too, to Gary's father, Barry, and to all the managers and players who offered their time and their views so readily. For the most part, that willingness was a pointer in itself to the enormous popularity of the man with his peers. Gary Lineker may be strikingly different from the average British footballer, but not so different that he has alienated himself from the other members of his somewhat rough-and-ready profession. Perhaps that is his greatest achievement of all.

· 1 ·

Home, Sweet Home

There is no way of knowing for sure what makes any of us what we are in terms of personality, character and occupation. As with the causes of criminality, it is difficult to determine whether hereditary factors or environmental influences are the more important. Geneticists and psychologists can make educated guesses, but apportioning the blame or the credit for how someone turns out cannot be an exact science. The subject is particularly fascinating with regard to professional football, an occupation in which surprisingly few sons of professional footballers are born with the talent and/or temperament to follow in their fathers' footsteps. It would seem that most top-class players are the offspring of keen footballers whose careers were confined to amateur or non-League levels: that the vital missing ingredient for success has been added somewhere along the line by genetic accident or through sheer hard work. Such is the case with Gary Lineker. It would be stretching the truth to say he was born to become one of the most expert and prolific goalscorers England has ever seen, but there is no doubt the right bloodlines were in place and that he did not want for encouragement and guidance at home.

There was never much doubt in the Linekers' Leicester household, during the late 1960s and early 1970s, that young Gary would become a professional footballer one day. Barry and Margaret, his father and mother, had so much faith in his potential that they even undertook a troublesome, inconvenient move of house to make sure their free-scoring son attended a soccer-playing school. 'We used to live in the city of Leicester,' explains Barry Lineker, 'but then we bought a house at Kirby Muxloe, which is in the country on the Leicester Forest East side, when Gary was about ten and his brother, Wayne, nine. We weren't thinking about schooling at the time. We just moved because we had found this nice house. We moved in, and then it was time for Gary to go to his senior school.

'The kids were at Caldecote Junior School, which wasn't far from where we actually moved to. But when Gary moved from Caldecote, he had to go to a county school, and the one he would have gone to didn't play soccer, they played rugby. Straightaway, I remembered that one of the biggest regrets I'd had in my life was going to a rugby school and not playing soccer for several years. So, we moved back into the city. Gary stayed with my mum and dad until such time as we had completed the move. In that way, his address became a city address and he could go to the City of Leicester Boys School, where they did play soccer. We were only in Kirby Muxloe for two years before we sold up and moved back. It shows how enthusiastic we were about his soccer career.'

That enthusiasm manifested itself every time Gary turned out for one of his school teams or for a local boys' club on Sundays. 'I used to go everywhere to watch him,' recalls his father with undisguised pride. 'I never missed a game when he was a kid – all his Sunday games and school games on a Saturday morning. He played for a local club, Aylestone Park, as well. They are still quite a big club in the city and he's honorary vice-president, or something like that. I think there's a big picture of him up in the club-house. He's their biggest claim to fame, I suppose. His grandad and I used to be on the touchline. I used to love it – it was great.'

Little wonder, since young Gary Winston Lineker (he was born on Winston Churchill's birthday, 30 November, in 1960, and hates his middle name) was scoring goals like a machine even then and was obviously a boy with a special talent. 'He was phenomenal as a kid,' says his father. 'He got an unbelievable amount of goals for whoever he played for. He really stood out, and he played for Leicester Boys all the way through his school career. Hat-tricks were ten-a-penny. He'd get a hat-trick every match, just about. Gary scored more than 200 goals one season for his school team and Aylestone Park. He was obviously exceptional, and we just hoped he would make the grade.'

Inevitably, it was not long before the scouts from League clubs both sides of the border were turning up to have a look at the Leicester prodigy. But it would be untrue to say they came in droves; in fact, the interest shown in him seemed at first glance to be much less great than his talent merited.

'There was a guy from Chelsea and a guy from Celtic, who

wanted him to go up to Glasgow,' Barry Lineker recalls. 'But we put him on schoolboy forms with Leicester City – I don't know whether that was a good move or not, and a lot of people said we shouldn't have done it – so I suppose that's why other clubs laid off.'

The man who made sure Leicester City did not lose Gary Lineker to one of their rivals was the late Ray Shaw, then chief scout at Filbert Street. There are conflicting stories about how the signing was actually made – whether or not Gary's grandfather, Harold, recommended him to Leicester. But Barry Lineker gives what he insists is the true version. 'Because my dad had been so involved in football all his life, he knew Ray Shaw,' he explains, 'and Ray came up to him to say hello one day when we were watching Gary play. My dad asked what he was doing there, and he said: "Oh, I've come to watch that young lad over there," pointing at Gary. "That's my grandson," replied my dad proudly. That's really how it happened, and Ray was the one who finished up signing Gary. A very nice man he was, too.'

Harold Lineker was a major influence on his talented grandson. The two of them were very close, and there is no doubt that Gary inherited some of his major assets from his grandfather, notably pace and an equable temperament. 'Gary takes after his grandad,' says Barry Lineker. 'He was very placid, too. I also understand that my dad was pretty quick when he was young. He played for Leicester Boys right through his school days and did actually have the chance to turn professional. But there was no money in it in those days, and his father wanted him to work in the family business. So that was it. He never really had the chance. He played for the Army, and I'm told he was very good. I never actually saw him myself. He was a right winger.'

Michelle Lineker, Gary's wife, was always struck by the similarities between Gary and his grandfather. 'He's a carbon copy of his grandad in terms of personality,' she has said. 'And I think we're just beginning to appreciate how good Grandad might have been if he'd had the same opportunities as a player.' A man reluctant to talk about himself, Harold Lineker was once persuaded to say: 'I never thought until recently that I must have been fairly decent. It's only through Gary that I've started thinking this. Nobody ever caught me if the ball was played in front of me, but it never struck me as anything special.'

After suffering from Parkinson's disease for many years, Harold Lineker died at the age of 80 in April 1992, just before Gary played for England against the CIS in Moscow, one of six pre-European Championship friendlies. So the Linekers had a second family tragedy to cope with in five months, following the discovery the previous November that Gary and Michelle's baby son, George, was suffering from acute myeloid leukaemia. 'To watch my father go down like he did was awful,' says Barry Lineker. 'You never know how long they've had Parkinson's disease before it starts to show, but we reckon he'd had it for something like 15 or 18 years.

'The last 12 months were horrible. He became a virtual cabbage. It was terrible. It's the most awful, awful complaint. He was almost unbelievably fit and healthy for his age. Unlike me, he didn't drink or smoke. So it was a terrible shame when he died. Towards the end, he couldn't feed himself or do anything for himself. My mum insisted that she wanted him at home, and we had a very, very good male nurse who used to come every night and put my dad to bed. He slept in the same room as him so that my mum could get a proper night's sleep. The nurse used to get him up in the morning and wash and dress him. He'd leave about 8–8.30 a.m. and then come back again in the evening.

'Gary paid for all that, which was very nice of him. He can afford it, obviously, but there was no hesitation. It was a case of: "I'll see to that." You are talking about quite a lot of money – the sort of thing ordinary people can't afford. It's just a pity that, in the last three or four years, my dad wasn't able to see Gary properly. He used to know Gary was on television – up until the last 12 months when he didn't know anything – but he'd watch the game and afterwards he didn't even know who'd scored. It just went out of his memory.'

Until he retired at 65, the greatly respected Harold Lineker (he was known as the 'Gentleman of Leicester market') had run the highly successful and long-established family business, G.A. Lineker & Son, a fruit and vegetable stall in Leicester's open-air market, the biggest permanent establishment of its kind in Europe. It houses about 500 stalls, one of which has been in the Lineker family for three generations. Founder of the business was Gary's great-grandfather, George Albert Lineker – no prizes for guessing one of the reasons for the name of Gary and Michelle's son – and Barry Lineker, now 53, has worked in it for 37 years himself. There must be some doubt, though, as to whether the direct family link will be continued. Gary can be ruled out completely. 'He's never shown any interest,' says his dad. 'He's helped us out the odd Saturday and the odd Christmas, but that's been about it, really. But he never had to. We always fancied he'd got a chance at football.' Brother Wayne has established his own business in Tenerife. It is a thriving bar called 'Lineker's', which Gary helped to get started.

They are an interesting pair, Gary and Wayne, and a fascinating contrast. Wayne, 17 months the younger, is Gary's complete opposite in many ways. Yet the bond between them is strong. 'They are different, and they are not,' explains their father. 'There are obvious similarities: both are excellent sportsmen, for a start. If you talk to anyone who has seen Wayne play football, they will tell you he should have made the grade as well. Wayne was tremendous; he had so much skill – a lot more than Gary. He had more dribbling ability and that sort of thing, whereas Gary is more direct and probably thinks more quickly. Wayne had a lot of talent, but he doesn't like discipline. I'm not saying he's a bad lad, or anything; it's just that he didn't like training. He liked to turn up, play and go home.

'When they were both going as youngsters to this training thing they had through Leicester City on Tuesday and Thursday nights, Wayne didn't want to bother, but Gary did. Basically, that's been it all the way through. So Wayne sort of drifted into the market with me and Gary went on to great things. I think Wayne's probably had some regrets, but I don't know. He's doing all right now with his bar in Tenerife. He's been there about four years. He never really took to the market that well. He did and didn't. He's always had aspirations to be wealthy, and he could see he wasn't going to be wealthy in the market. It's a good living, and that's all. Now he's on the way to what he wants, I think.

'With hindsight, Wayne probably wishes he had been more dedicated. But there's never been any jealousy because Gary's made it. Wayne's always been Gary's number one fan. If I wasn't going, or his grandfather wasn't, Wayne would go anywhere to watch Gary play. Nobody could say anything against his brother, and they are good mates. Gary helped him with the bar out in Spain, to get him off the ground. They are very close, and always have been.'

Like his grandfather, but unlike Gary, Wayne always played on the wing. He is also much taller than his brother – 6ft 2in as against Gary's 5ft 10in – and slower. 'Lack of pace was probably one of the things that held Wayne back in the early days,' says Barry Lineker. 'But his stride is tremendous, and it helped to make up for his lack of speed. He was quick once he got going, but not off the mark. If he'd stayed with it, though, I'm sure he'd have made it.'

Another problem, and another contrast with his brother, was Wayne's volatile temperament. 'Wayne flared up very easily,' admits his father, 'and I suppose he takes after me. I used to be a bit that way.'

Barry Lineker never played in anything more exalted than local non-League football, and you sense a certain amount of frustration about it. 'We had a Thursday League, which was a trades league,' he says. 'It doesn't exist any more, unfortunately, because the old tradition of half-days doesn't exist any more. I used to play for our market side in that league. It was quite a good standard of football, really. There were some good sides in it. I played football when I was young, but then I went to a school that only played rugby. I never took to rugby very much, and I never played soccer between the ages of 11 and 16 – till I left school, in fact. So if I had any talent, it was never going to show because it was too late. There was no Sunday football then, of course. So if you didn't play at school, you didn't play. I always regretted it, not having any school football, because I was very quick, too. But whether I was good enough to have done anything, I don't know. It never amounted to anything.'

One thing Barry Lineker did do was make sure his sons learned to kick with both feet. 'I played inside-left,' he says, 'and I'm naturally left-footed. Both boys are two-footed because I made them kick with both feet when they were kids. It's been the most important thing. There have been some marvellous one-footed players, but I wonder how much better they would have been with two good feet. Wayne became so good with his left foot, he used to play on the left wing. Though he was a natural right-footer, his left became better than his right. It's a big advantage if you can use both feet.'

Lineker senior also passed on a love of the game and of the local club to his sons. 'Our family's always been sports-mad,' he says. 'I've supported Leicester City all my life, and Gary and Wayne both had season-tickets from when they were about eight. They used to go down to Filbert Street with us every Saturday. It was a great thrill when Leicester decided to take Gary on as an apprentice. I think there were 13 apprentices signed that year, and Gary was the only one who made the grade. There's still a long way to go when you get that far.

'Although Leicester wasn't that fashionable a club at the time, I think it's better if kids can be at home at that stage in their careers. So many of them have gone wrong through going away to another club. George Best is a classic example. I always think of him in this context because he came over here from Northern Ireland a raw lad of 16. He didn't know anything about the world and was alone over here. I think a lot of the blame's got to be put on Manchester United. They never looked after him like they should have done. I know it's not easy, but I always think it's very, very sad that we never saw enough of the best of George Best.

'I think it was just that he was away from home and in the lime-light. Suddenly, from being nobody at 16, he was famous in all the papers and I suppose he just couldn't handle it. He hadn't got any-body to put a hand on his shoulder and say: "Steady on, George!" Whereas if kids are living at home they are probably not going to indulge in the temptations that are undoubtedly there because they know their parents are not going to stand for it. I'm not trying to take any of the credit, but I firmly believe that it's a big advantage for a kid if he can play for his home club to start with. Obviously, it's been a good decision in Gary's case because he's stayed level-headed. At the time the temptations were there he was at home and it never came to anything. If he'd started stepping out of line a bit, I would have jumped on him. But I never had to, fortunately.

'Away from home, you are always at a loose end, and the other lads say: "Come on, let's go down the disco", or whatever. We all know how alluring temptations can be, especially when you are on your own. So, Gary sunk himself into snooker, and that's where he spent all his spare time – in Willie Thorne's snooker club. It kept him out of trouble, he enjoyed it and he became big friends with Willie. Gary became a very good snooker player, too. He got century breaks regularly: 130-odd was his highest, I think. He's just a natural ball-player.'

It is almost a case of you name it, and Gary Lineker plays it. Cricket, of course, has always been his other great sporting love. As a boy, he was a regular at Leicestershire's indoor coaching sessions, and the club clearly harboured hopes that he would decide to pur-sue a career in county cricket. But Barry Lineker was never in any doubt that his son would opt for soccer. 'It never really transpired that Gary was going to play cricket professionally. I think soccer has always been the one thing he wanted to do, but I do believe he could have made the grade at cricket. He played in a David Gower testimonial a couple of years ago, and he got a hundred or close on it. That was against professionals. I mean, he doesn't have any nets: he just goes out and plays! He captained Leicestershire Schoolboys at cricket. He played all the way through at that level, cricket and football. He was also a good athlete. The 100 metres was his forte – the 400 as well. He was quite a good golfer, too, when he was playing regularly; but he doesn't play as much as he would like now. I suppose when he comes back from Japan, that's what he'll be doing – plenty of golf, plenty of cricket.'

It seems odd now to think that Gary Lineker was so small and skinny when he joined Leicester City from school (under 5ft 6in and less than nine stone) that manager Jock Wallace, a tough, strapping Scotsman who liked his players to be made of reinforced concrete, thought him too frail to continue as a striker and played him on the wing. 'He was a late developer physically,' says Barry Lineker, 'and I think playing on the wing held his career back for a little while. But eventually he forced his way through, and Jock realised that a striker is what he really was.

'He did do some weight training, and Leicester asked us to put him on a special diet. We used to get him steak every week, fish and that sort of thing. But nothing extra-special, really. He was just a late developer. He was still probably growing when he was 19, whereas some kids have finished at 16. I was the same. I was very small when I was at school. I grew from about 16 to 18, shot up then, and Gary was probably the same. We are very much alike in that sense.'

He had also left school with a dire warning from his headmaster at the City of Leicester Boys School ringing in his ears. In one report, the head had complained that Lineker was not paying enough attention to his school-work and predicted, with spectacular inaccuracy, that he could not expect to earn his living playing football. But Barry Lineker insists that Gary is quite bright, a claim supported strongly by his son's subsequent mastery of foreign languages and media disciplines, and could have emerged with a better academic record than he did. 'I suppose his sport was more important than his school-work,' says the father, 'but he did well at school. He got four O-levels, I think, and could probably have got more. He didn't have to work very hard because things come very easily to Gary. He's quite intelligent and he learns quickly. He just sailed through school, really. He never had a lot of problems.'

Just as Barry Lineker was adamant that Gary should begin his career with Leicester, he sensed when the moment had come for his son to leave. 'There was no way he could have stayed at Leicester any longer,' he says. 'He'd been there for nine years anyway, counting the schoolboy period. He had to move on, and the Everton move was brilliant. It was out of the blue. I just got a 'phone call: "Dad, I'm going to Everton." You're joking, I thought. I suppose I was a bit disappointed when he went to Barcelona, because I still wonder what he could have achieved if he'd stayed another couple of years at Everton. But it was a tremendous move, going to Barcelona, and I think he came back a better player. He learned a lot out there.'

While Barry and Margaret Lineker – now divorced – always expected Gary to make the grade as a footballer, they never, in their wildest dreams anticipated quite how rich and famous he would become. 'We all have aspirations for our kids, don't we,' says Barry, 'but we could never have imagined he was going to finish up as captain of England, be leading scorer in the World Cup finals and win four Golden Boots, plus a Silver one with Leicester in the Second Division.

'He's not been affected by it all, either. I'm probably as proud of what he's become through his fame as I am of his fame, if you understand what I mean. He's always handled himself very well, and it's never gone to his head. Obviously it's changed his lifestyle, and obviously he's worth a lot of money now – though I haven't got a clue how much. But he's worked hard for it, and he deserves it. The nicest thing of all, though, is that it hasn't affected him the tiniest bit, and he is still the same person he was when he left school and was just starting to make his way in the world.'

Conscious, no doubt, of the break-up of his own marriage and that of his younger son, a rather messy business chronicled in one of the Sunday tabloids, Barry Lineker obviously delights in the success of the union between Gary and Michelle. It certainly amuses him to recall that the two families, the Linekers and the Cockaynes, knew each other well before Gary and Michelle ever met. 'Michelle's father is managing director of Broadbents, a Leicester roofing company, and the connection is that Michelle's grandmother lives next door to my mum,' he explains. 'So when he came home and told us about this girl he'd met, we knew who it was, of course. We didn't think much would come of it, but I'm very happy it did. Michelle's a lovely girl, and they are a nice family. That's good to know, especially in this day and age. They both like the same things – living in London and the adventure of living abroad.'

Barry Lineker admits that the split with his ex-wife, after 24 years of marriage, was 'a bit traumatic' for Gary and Wayne, who were in their early twenties at the time. 'Fortunately,' he adds, 'they were old enough to handle it.' Since then, Margaret Lineker has re-married and lives in a houseboat on the Thames. Barry has not got quite as far as tying the knot again, but has lived happily with a lady antique dealer in the Leicester area for the past nine years. It is an arrangement that seems to work well enough so far as Gary and his parents are concerned. His mother is close by in London, and he keeps in touch with his father on a regular basis.

'We go occasionally to see Gary and Michelle in London,' says Barry Lineker, a self-confessed hater of the capital city, 'but a lot of that was curtailed, of course, with the baby being so ill. We went down a couple of times, but you couldn't just walk in and see George because they had to restrict access to him. We've seen quite a bit of him since, though; Gary and Michelle brought him up here on his first birthday, for example. Obviously, I don't see as much of them as I'd like, but we speak on the 'phone quite a lot. Gary and I are more like mates, really, than father and son. It's the same with Wayne as well. We all get on famously, and that's nice, I think.'

Now Barry Lineker is looking forward to going out to see his son extend a remarkable career in Japan. 'I think he's got a bit of a deal with British Airways for family and friends,' he confides con-spiratorially. Nagoya Grampus Eight is a long way from Caldecote Junior School and Aylestone Park in more ways than one, but there can be little doubt that the strength of Gary Lineker's family ties has helped carry him through all the challenges he has taken on, and met so successfully, along the way.

Although Barry Lineker cannot say it for himself, Gary's family background clearly has something to do with all the admirable traits he carried into adulthood. Mark Wallington, the former Leicester goalkeeper and captain, puts it like this: 'Even from 16, Gary's always had a sound background and upbringing in the sense that he had his feet on the floor with his grandparents and his father being market people. He's known what life's about, never walked around with his head in the clouds. Whichever task he's been given, at whatever stage in his career, he's buckled down to it and got on with it.'

· 2 ·

Jonathan Holmes –
Special Agent

No-one – manager, coach or player – has exerted more influence on Gary Lineker's career than his agent, Jonathan Holmes. There is little doubt that, given the player's natural talent, driving ambition and native intelligence, he would have made his mark in professional football without any assistance from Holmes. It is less certain, however, that Lineker would have come to enjoy the special place in the affection of the public he enjoys today if he had not had the good fortune to encounter his Svengali while a novice professional with Leicester City.

Holmes himself disagrees strongly with my flattering interpretation of his role and suggests his client probably would, too. Nevertheless, it is impossible to ignore the fact that he is the man responsible for creating Lineker's world-famous 'Roy of the Rovers' image, a squeaky-clean identity worth millions of pounds in endorsements. It was quite deliberate, as Holmes himself readily admits: this was a conscious exercise in global marketing. Getting the image exactly right, he claims convincingly, was more important to him than making lots of money out of it – but one follows on from the other, of course.

This unusual tendency to regard short-term profit as being less important than projecting exactly the right image for his clients is, to a large extent, what sets Holmes apart from most other practitioners of his widely reviled trade. 'Agent' has become a dirty word in professional football over the past decade, mainly because of this middle-man's interference in the financial and contractual relationship between player and club, but little of the mud has stuck to Holmes.

That is because, as a devoted football fan, he does make a conscious effort to act in the best interests of the game as well as of his clients. It is a toss-up whether upgrading the status of the professional footballer or improving the state of the English game comes first in his order of priorities. His reward, as he sees it, has been harmonious relationships with almost all the managers of the footballers he advises. Most of them would probably testify, however, that Holmes's philanthropic attitude to the game does not extend to the negotiating table.

Nobody's fool, this good-naturedly frank and hearty East Midlander has one distinct advantage over most of his competitors – a sharp mind polished by a good education. Public school (Oundle) was followed by Leeds University, where Holmes read Politics and graduated in the early 1970s with a second class honours degree. He also worked on the university newspaper, an experience that helped fuel an ambition to become a sports writer.

'I wanted to be a journalist at that stage,' he recalls. 'Perhaps it wasn't surprising that we won an award: the editor at that time was Paul Dacre, now editor of the *Daily Mail*, and the features editor, a fellow I worked with quite a lot, was David Durman, now editor of *Woman*. It was fairly illustrious stuff.'

However, the glamour soon wore off after leaving Leeds. An unhappy year on his local paper, the *Leicester Mercury*, as a general news reporter left Holmes disillusioned and looking for a new career. He considers it anything but wasted experience, though. 'It gave me a little bit of insight,' he says, 'and I've always enjoyed the company of journalists and the ethos of journalism. I think a lot of people in my job don't understand where journalists come from, if you know what I mean. Therefore, they always end up having problems with them.'

On leaving the *Mercury*, Holmes moved into the financial services business. His boss, who had heard of the legendary American sports agent, Mark McCormack, and thereby went up in his new employee's estimation, had a connection with football and encouraged Holmes to begin advising local sportsmen such as Peter Shilton, by then Nottingham Forest's goalkeeper, and David Gower, then a Leicestershire cricketer, as a sideline. Eventually, that part of the business grew large enough for Holmes, encouraged by Shilton and another of his early clients, Tony Woodcock, the former Forest and England striker, to go it alone.

'I did sort of half-and-half at that point,' he explains, 'and then it developed so that I'm now doing this [advising and representing sportsmen] all the time; although I do still have a few financial services clients. It gives me some awareness of the investment angle and importance of money – what it can and can't do.'

Holmes now operates out of an elegant Georgian building in the centre of Nottingham. It houses both his sports management business, Park Associates, and a financial services company, Benson McGarvey, which his partner, Peter McGarvey, runs. 'I'm still a partner in the other bit,' he explains, 'and Peter's a director of my bit. We offer my sports clients a complete financial package, but they have their own lawyers and accountants. A lot of my time is spent talking with accountants because I can speak their language. Players sometimes find it difficult to talk to accountants, and vice-versa, so I act as a middle-man.

'I had read Mark McCormack's book on Arnold Palmer at university, and was interested in the idea of a sportsman using the sport to do other things and, conversely, the sport using the sportsman to promote itself. Stars are what sport needs, and the major players are the major salesmen. Therefore, they need to be looked after. It amazes me that the marketing ability of a lot of people who run sport is appalling in terms of the way they actually treat the major 'salesmen'. There isn't another industry in the world like soccer, where the players still call the manager 'Boss' or 'Gaffer'. It's a joke, isn't it? A sort of throwback to the days of Victorian mill owners.'

The high-class 'stable' of leading sportsmen Holmes now runs includes four other footballers – John Barnes (Liverpool and England), Neil Webb (Manchester United and England), Gary McAllister (Leeds United and Scotland) and Lee Chapman (Leeds United) – two cricketers, Gower (now Hampshire and, when they are in the mood, England) and Mike Atherton (Lancashire and England), plus Will Carling, captain of the England rugby team. Holmes also 'does a bit', he says, for Leicester and England rugby winger Rory Underwood, promising middle-distance runner Matthew Yates and two former sporting luminaries, athlete Sebastian Coe and swimmer Adrian Moorhouse. Even so, Gary Lineker remains the star attraction and principal money-spinner.

The initial meeting between Holmes and Lineker took place in 1980, but it would be untrue to say they hit it off at once. 'When Gary first came to see me,' Holmes recalls, 'he came about pensions. I used to look after the financial affairs of the younger players at Leicester City, and he was brought in to see me as one of the young-sters who wanted to start a pension scheme. He came in with Andy Peake [a midfielder once regarded as a better prospect than Lineker, who has spent the rest of his career in relative obscurity with Grimsby, Charlton and Middlesbrough], but he said hardly a word. All he did was nod in agreement, grunt "Yes" and so on.

'It seemed to me he was a very shy lad. To be honest, Peakey had a lot more about him at that stage. They were quite good mates and quite good cricketers. I didn't really have much more to do with Gary because I was quite pressed at the time; but he gradually improved and improved as a player. I can remember having a conversation with Mark Wallington [the former Leicester City goalkeeper and captain] driving home from Filbert Street one night. We were talking about the younger players, and Mark agreed with me that Gary had improved a lot.

'During Wally's [Wallington's] testimonial year, Gary was brilliant – he'd go to everything and do everything – and it gradually dawned on me that he was one of those people who had more about them than was immediately obvious. I took a bit more interest in him, and eventually a mate of mine, who knew Gary's mother, said to me, "You ought to go and get him formally tied up, you know, because his family are keen for you to look after him and he's doing quite well."

'So I went to have a chat with his parents and told them I'd like to look after him. I remember saying at the time that it would be five years before he made any money. That was about right, but his father says now, "You never knew how much money!" which was also true. There was a match later that season against Wolves. Gary only scored one goal, but he was terrific and I came to the conclusion then that he would be a very good player.

'In those early days I would have lunch with him about once a month. We'd just chat about things in general. I think he understands what I do, and I understand the way he thinks. We generally agree on things. He's from a roughly similar background to mine, in that he's from a business family in Leicester. We've got interests in common – cricket and golf, for example – so we've always got on well. We do talk quite a bit and enjoy each other's company. I think you have to be reasonably close to people to advise them on personal finance. In Gary's case, I've had more contact with him than with anybody else. We've got a similar sense of humour so it's always worked quite well. He doesn't have rows, anyway. I'll say to him, "You're not happy about that, are you?" and he'll say, "No, I'm not." But that's about as far as we'll go in that respect. We do know how to deal with each other.

'After he had played two seasons in the (old) First Division, I advised him on his contract. I told him to extend it for just one year, because he was on 'nothing' money [£10–15,000 a year]. We upped his wages a little bit, but I didn't think he should extend the contract beyond the one year because, as I told him, it would be in his best interests to move on as quickly as possible after that.'

There followed the moves, most of them rewarding professionally as well as financially, to Everton, Barcelona, Tottenham Hotspur and Grampus Eight. Each time, Holmes was at the centre of things, advising on the suitability of the would-be purchasers and, as a hard-nosed negotiator, getting round a table with the bidders to thrash out the financial details of the transfer. All the time, too, he was steadily strengthening the image of Gary Lineker, paragon of virtue, footballer with a difference.

'You look for role models,' says Holmes, beginning to explain how he set about promoting Lineker so successfully as a 'Boy's Own' hero. 'I'd always regarded Arnold Palmer highly, especially in terms of how he'd been able to market himself. With Gary I couldn't have wished for better material; all I do is emphasise certain points.

'I wanted him to be respected personally, and I wanted footballers in general to be regarded in a different light from before. People always say Gary's very bright and intelligent – and he is – but he's got fewer academic qualifications than a lot of other players.

'I encouraged him to talk more to the serious newspapers. A lot of players say the *Sun* and the *Star* are an absolute scandal, but if you ask them what newspapers they take at home, they say: "The *Sun* or the *Star*." They complain they are a complete waste of time, yet spend all their time reading them. I also advised Gary to appear on different types of television programmes. I told him he'd find the most in-depth ones more rewarding. And I encouraged him to read more, but he would do that sort of thing anyway because he wanted to. He didn't want to be regarded as a 'thicko.' I don't think most people do, but half the time they don't give themselves a chance. You've got to get away from the stereotype.'

Inevitably, after more than a decade together, the relationship between Holmes and Lineker goes beyond that of agent and client. But it always did, given that Holmes' own hopes and dreams were bound up with Lineker's from the start. 'It was my ambition, when I went into this business, to take someone as far as I have Gary,' he admits. 'He helped me realise an ambition for myself. We both know that.'

Holmes concedes that he enjoyed considerable luck in finding such an ideal person as Lineker for the undertaking. 'If you dreamt up what you thought a footballer ought to be like, Gary probably fits the mould perfectly. He's a centre-forward; he's articulate and he's intelligent; he's made himself. What is different about him, really, is that he's had the common sense to use the game to broaden himself. He's an example of the university of life, isn't he?

'He left school at 16 with about four O-levels, I think. His school reports suggest he was all right academically, but I suspect he didn't try too hard. There's not a great academic background in the family at all. There was a sporting and business background, and they weren't poor. He's a middle-class footballer to that extent, in fact. People hear his father runs a greengrocery stall in Leicester market and think Gary is a barrow-boy, or something. But that's far from being the case.

'The stall has been in the family for generations. They lived in quite a decent middle-class residential area. The interesting thing is that, the further Gary's career has gone, the more he's developed. I was talking to Brian Barwick [Editor of BBC TV's *Match of The Day* and *Sportsnight*] about the stuff he's done on television. Some of it was very good, some not quite so brilliant. But Brian said he will be brilliant in the finish because of his attitude and the way he gets on with things. He's right, because Gary sets himself realistic targets and gets there.

'He's not frightened of taking on new challenges, either. Sometimes he's said: "Oh, I don't know whether I could do that." But he's had a go at it. What I like to be is an encourager. I say to people: "Yeah, I think you can do that!" and then enjoy watching them prove to themselves they can do it. The invitation to speak at the Oxford Union came into that category. Gary said at first: "You'll want me to do this, but I'm not too sure." In other words, he was half-saying to me: "Persuade me to do it."

'So I said: "Yeah, of course we'll do it! There's no problem." In other words, just another bit of encouragement. When he asked me how we were going to put together a speech – the motion, if I remember rightly, was "Better to Participate than to Commentate?" – I said: "Well, we can put this bit in and that bit in. I'll get Stan Hey [the television scriptwriter and sports journalist] to help us."

'Stan put down a speech and Gary fiddled about with it. I flung in the odd bit, and Gary worked on it and rehearsed it and proved to himself he could do it. He proved he could go into the Oxford

Union and not be looked upon as a moron. He did have the good grace to say to me afterwards: "It has to be said, that was one of your better ideas!" As you can see, we don't overdo it and tell each other how clever we are all of the time.'

Nor, without doubt, how rich they are. They must have made an awful lot of money along the way, but it is a subject upon which Holmes prefers to touch only lightly. The reason, almost certainly, is that it does not square with the carefully cultivated Lineker image. He admits, almost diffidently, that, yes, Gary is probably a millionaire, then hedges his assessment with qualifications. 'It depends how you value houses. He is a millionaire, I suppose, if you take net assets.'

Those assets include a palatial Regency home in the up-market St John's Wood area of London – handy for Lord's cricket ground and valued in 1992 at £800,000 – and 'other property and interests'. Then, of course, there are the substantial sums Lineker has collected in signing-on fees and wages from his transfers to Everton, Barcelona and Tottenham. And the biggest pay-day of the lot has still to come from the move to Grampus Eight, of Japan. But, as Holmes insists, to dwell on Lineker's undoubted wealth is to miss the point about his success.

'Gary's not just concerned with money,' argues his agent. 'OK, so he's done well financially, but it's never been the total aim. I've never sought to justify my position by saying I'll make more money for my clients than anyone else. It's like being the fastest gun in the West. If I'm totally honest, I have to say that other people might have made my clients more money than I have. It's short-term versus long-term: who's to say which is better? Someone told me quite early in business: "Never marry for money, marry where money is." In other words, shape things to the general area you want to be in.

'Personally, I don't define success just in terms of money. I think it's important, but if you regard it as the only thing, you'll end up unhappy because someone earns more. I think I've done OK financially for my clients: I'm not a mug. But I also know the kind of money we are talking about is actually peanuts compared to what is possible in other fields. I mean, we've got a client on the financial services side of the business who sold out for £50 million the other week. Now that makes footballers' earnings look pretty insignificant.'

In truth, Holmes makes his relationship with Lineker sound more like a crusade than a business partnership. An innocent enquiry about the date of the Lineker's marriage suddenly sparks off a tirade about the social standing of professional footballers that reveals much about the man and his motivation.

'They got married just after the 1986 World Cup,' he begins, 'but they had been going out for two or three years by then. As long as I've been involved with Gary, Michelle has been around.

'She was a beauty therapist. It doesn't sound like a great meeting of minds, does it? A beauty therapist and a footballer! But they don't fit the mould at all. He's broken the mould, and the mould was something that always irked me. I got interested in soccer because my father was very keen and always took me to the matches. But I went to a public school, a rugby school, and football was always regarded in a patronising way.

'That always annoyed me and, in a way, I've enjoyed the fact that Gary's now regarded as something different. I deliberately turned him, in the public's eyes, into a cricketer. [Take Lineker's well-documented playing membership of MCC, for example.] That's because people always said to me: "Oh, cricketers are more intelligent than footballers." That's a stupid generalisation, of course. It's only true in the way they are treated. It's unsurprising that most footballers sound awful when they go on TV or radio, because there's no encouragement anywhere to better themselves. They [the football establishment] don't want them to get involved.'

In Lineker's case, Holmes can regard his crusade as extremely successful. No footballer has been in greater demand by the media. During his 'sabbatical' between the end of the European Championship finals in June 1992 and his departure for Japan in February 1993, Lineker was hardly off the airwaves. A trip to the Barcelona Olympics as a member of the BBC TV commentary team was followed, on his return, by regular appearances on the resurrected *Match of the Day*, still Britain's most popular TV football programme, and a weekly football programme of his own, *Gary Lineker's Football Night*, on Radio Five.

You can add to that, of course, the OBE Lineker was awarded in the 1992 New Year's Honours List, two honorary degrees – from Leicester and Loughborough universities – an appearance on Desert Island Discs, a West End play entitled *An Evening With Gary Lineker* (in which the player is depicted as 'The Queen Mother of football') and, perhaps the greatest accolade of them all, a standing ovation from the hard-bitten English football writers at the end of the press conference the day after his substitution against Sweden in Stockholm.

Then, in August 1992, came the final, legal proof that Lineker was a national institution. At Newport Crown Court, the sort of place where questions like: 'What exactly is a Gazza?' are liable to be asked, Judge John Prosser recommended that an amateur footballer, Ian Jolosa, should watch videos of Gary Lineker in action. Giving centre-forward Jolosa, 28, an 18-month conditional discharge for hitting an opponent so hard he broke his jaw, Judge Prosser said: 'Lineker has never been sent off. You must look at film of him and do all you can to emulate his behaviour.'

Jolosa preferred not to take the advice and soon got himself into hot water again. 'I treated the judge's words as a bit of a joke,' he said cockily, 'I prefer action films. If Lineker played in the same leagues as I do, then he would end up in the same trouble.' But leading English referee David Elleray is one of many who would probably disagree. 'He has great skill at keeping out of trouble when trouble is going on,' observed Elleray. 'He just doesn't get involved. He neither provokes nor reacts; rather like a British diplomat, I'd say. He's got a very stable temperament. He's worked out that dissent doesn't do any good.'

While such remarkable forbearance has certainly enhanced the player's image, there have been more tangible rewards as well. In December 1991, FIFA recognised Lineker's 'exemplary conduct' by awarding him the coveted Fair Play trophy, which is worth £25,000 and had been given to an individual player only once previously. The FIFA commendation said they considered him 'a living example of how the spirit of fair play can be crowned with personal success.' Lineker, for his part, promptly donated half his winnings to a Leicester charity treating children with cancer.

A man who finds it difficult to take himself too seriously, he adopts a typically self-mocking attitude to his whiter-than-white image. 'I think, in the last couple of minutes of my last game, I might just go up and smack the ref on the jaw,' joked the Nicest Man on Earth, the sobriquet given him by the Tottenham fanzine, *Spur*, as he neared the end of his career in English football. 'As far as I'm concerned, you could have a worse image. I'm not particularly worried about it, though it does get a bit goody-goody and a bit sickening at times. A few things get embarrassing, but I know what I'm really like and my family know what I'm really like: very, very sickeningly goody-goody. But I'd sooner be like that than the other way round, with people saying how awful I was.'

No-one can get through life without making a few enemies, but it is not easy to find them in Gary Lineker's case. Much more common than criticism is the kind of heartfelt tribute offered by Mark Wallington. 'Knowing the lad personally,' he says, 'his career is a triumph for the nice guy. He's not the idiot centre-forward who's got to head-butt the goalkeeper into the net. He's proved that nice guys can make it right to the top. Look round now at the way people behave and it really is distressing. I'm so chuffed for the boy. He's a genuine, caring character and he's not pretentious or anything like that.

'He's Mr Clean, he's never done anything wrong. But that's the way the lad is, and good luck to him. I tell you what, in a profession that's quite filthy from top to bottom – you know, you've got to be a little bit hard, be able to kick out and fight your corner – the man has been able to keep his head well above it and say, "I'm going to do it my way". And he has. He's a quality lad.'

And what of the future for Holmes himself? Since expansion seems to be the name of his game, does he see himself as a latter-day Mark McCormack perhaps? 'No, I'm not as ambitious as he is,' he protests. 'I'm ambitious for my clients, but not in a monetary sense. I'd be more interested in them getting something out of it. My ambition now is to have clients in a lot of different sports. Will Carling's been an interesting departure for me.'

Part of the trick in getting on with leading sportsmen, Holmes reckons, is 'treating people as ordinary although they are special. You have to acknowledge that they are special, but at the same time they remain ordinary people.' His sense of humour would not suit everyone, however. 'I'll take the piss out of people at that level,' he avers. 'Gower's always said I'd last about five minutes with Ian Botham because of it.' But then again, who could ever imagine Botham, the erstwhile wild man of cricket, applying to become whiter-than-white? Come to that, who could see Holmes inviting him? Gary Lineker rules, OK?

· 3 ·

Leicester – The Seed Bed

Gary Lineker was introduced to top-class English football in circumstances just about as far removed from his glamorous future as can be imagined. The weather was cold and the conditions icy when he made his first-team debut for Leicester City in a Second Division match against Oldham Athletic at Filbert Street on New Year's Day, 1979. Leicester won 2–0 but Lineker, just turned 18 and playing on the right wing in the number seven shirt usually worn by former England international Keith Weller, did not score and made little impression. 'He was absolute crap, to be honest,' says Jon Holmes, who actually watched his famous client-to-be's inauspicious debut. Star of the show that day was David Buchanan, a 16-year-old apprentice, who scored one of Leicester's two goals and overshadowed all the other youngsters the club's bristling new manager, Jock Wallace, had brought in for this match.

A devout believer in the efficacy of youth, Wallace had decided to shake up a Leicester team sliding towards the bottom of the Second Division after being relegated from the First the previous season. It worked, too. Eventually, the East Midlands club finished in the comparative safety of seventeenth position. Our hero had very little to do with that, though. Lineker was not picked again for the first team until the following April, although he did keep his place for the final six games of the season once he got in. He also – a very important milestone this – scored the first of the 236 League goals he was to register in 439 appearances. It was the winner in a 1–0 victory at Notts County on 24 April, 1979, his fourth game for Leicester.

Typically, he remembers it well. 'Mick Duffy crossed the ball, and I scored with a right-foot volley from just a few yards out with a few minutes left. There weren't many games left and we needed a win to stay in the Second Division. I thought for a while it was going to be my last goal as well.' Lineker did not score again until 13 games into the following season, when he claimed both of Leicester's goals in a 2–0 win against Sunderland. There was only one more goal to come in his 19 appearances that season, but any personal disappointment was offset by Leicester's success in going back up to the First Division as Second Division champions. For a time, though, it looked as if the step up in class might be too big for Lineker to take.

He found it hard to command a regular first-team place and did not make his First Division debut until 8 October, 1980, in a 1–1 draw at home with Stoke City. He scored in his next game, against Coventry City, and again against West Bromwich Albion the following month, but Leicester were slipping back down towards the Second Division once more. Relegated in twenty-first position, they found themselves without their first-choice striker, Scotsman Alan Young, because of injury at the start of the following season. Young's loss was Lineker's gain. Included from the opening day, and operating in partnership with the experienced Scot, Jim Melrose, Lineker scored in his first game, a 2–2 draw at Grimsby, and went on to finish the season as the club's leading scorer with 17 League goals in 39 appearances. Suddenly, he had exploded. He collected another two goals as Leicester reached the semi-finals of the FA Cup, where they lost 2–0 to the Tottenham Hotspur of Glenn Hoddle and Ossie Ardiles. Leicester also finished eighth in the Second Division, so it was something of a shock when the abrasive, but popular, Jock Wallace announced he was leaving to join Motherwell because he felt the need to return to his native Scotland.

Enter Gordon Milne, the quiet, thoughtful manager who decided to pair Lineker with Alan Smith, a £15,000 signing from non-League Alvechurch and Jock Wallace's last buy for Leicester. They hit it off so well that they scored 39 League goals between them, Lineker supplying 26 from 40 games and again finishing as the club's leading scorer. His first hat-trick came on 11 September, 1982, when Carlisle were beaten 6–0 at Filbert Street, and there was a second one the following month in a 4–0 victory at Derby. Leicester, promoted to the First Division in third place, were flying high and Lineker was beginning to attract the attention of bigger, wealthier clubs.

One Leicester player who watched this transformation with interest, pleasure and not a little disbelief was Mark Wallington, the club's goalkeeper and captain for most of the 14 seasons he spent at Filbert Street between 1971 and 1985.

'I'd seen him when he was introduced into the side by Jock Wallace,' recalls Wallington, now retired from the game and happily teaching PE in his birthplace, Sleaford, Lincs. 'Jock introduced Gary, Neil Grewcock and Dave Buchanan – all of them teenagers. We'd been relegated the previous year and Jock had a big clear-out. He went for youth to such an extent that he was bringing in young lads left, right and centre. At that time, Neil, Dave and Gary were forwards, all very small, all very quick. Dave Buchanan was the most impressive of the three and this continued for a while as regards play.

'At that age, Gary had tremendous acceleration and the positional sense to score goals; but when it came to linking play, you'd avoid giving him the ball. I mean, he'd just stand there! But as soon as we realised how quick he was, we were knocking balls on the inside of full-backs, or down the side of centre-backs, and releasing Gary. In the Second Division, a lot of the centre-halves are either not quite good enough for the First Division, or are coming back down to the Second because they've lost their pace. So we exploited it that way. His pace was such that he could allow people a couple of yards' start and still get in front of them. The beauty of it, for the midfield or the full-backs, was that if the ball went long, or was hit into the corners, you knew he'd have the pace to get there. If it was a more direct through-ball along the deck – a very incisive ball – you knew he'd be quick enough to get on to it before anyone could cut it out. So the options he gave lads on the ball were terrific.

'But it was his knack of putting the ball in the net at speed that attracted a lot of clubs to him. When I was skipper at Leicester – and I'm sure Gary won't mind me saying this – I was asked by a friend if I thought he would move. I think the bids were knocking on £350,000–£400,000 at the time, and I said: "Come the first offer of £500,000, and I'd sell him." That's because I could only see him as a pace man. I thought that once he lost his acceleration, got a couple of heavy knocks on the legs and started to get knee trouble, he wouldn't have anything left. So far as I was concerned, he couldn't head a ball or trap a ball. All he had was electric pace and an eye for goal. He'd been our leading scorer for two years at that stage, and I said I thought any manager worth his salt would get rid of him for £500,000.

'What happened after that was a delight to see. He moved to

Everton the same year as I went to Derby, and he seemed to mature then, get stronger and begin to hold the ball up a wee bit more. Howard Kendall had obviously seen the potential there and paid – what was it – £800,000 for him, which was absolutely brilliant for Leicester. When I saw him a year later working up at Everton with better players and better coaching, the whole set-up, he was different class. From then on, he never looked back. But I must admit I honestly thought that, once he started getting clobbered, he'd stop developing. So you can imagine how I felt when, in his first season at Everton, he scored a lot of goals with his head: near post, good positional sense, attacking the ball, a lot stronger. To me, it was a revelation how he'd developed, and I was absolutely delighted.

'Obviously, I never imagined he'd become the internationally famous footballer he is today. All he had for me was electric pace and good goalscoring ability; but his linking play – which has become a very important part of his game, dropping off into the midfield and all that – has been developed over the years under some terrific managers like Howard Kendall and Terry Venables. He had to move from Leicester to get that coaching. He'd never have got it there. A lot of it's to do with what's between the ears, of course, and I think Gary's developed terrifically well by applying his mind to the game. You often get lads that'll have two or three good seasons, then blow. Alan Young, for instance, was an exceptional player Leicester bought from Oldham for £350,000. For two seasons, Alan was absolutely superb. He was strong in the air, he was quick, good left foot, not a bad right one. But after two seasons, he'd blown it. His mentality wasn't right. But Gary's got the mentality to say, "Right. I'll do this and I'll do that: that's how I'm going to work it."

'It's a pity Jock wasn't there to see Gary and Alan Smith together, because Jock was a great admirer of Gary's. He loved young players, he really did. He had no hesitation at all about chucking them in. I remember one match where we could have been relegated to the Third Division – it was against Sheffield United at Bramall Lane – and he threw in about six lads under 18. I said to him afterwards, "You took a hell of a chance there, Gaffer, didn't you?" And he said, "Look, we are going to have to rely on them next year, and I've learned more about them tonight than I would in half a season." That was his philosophy. Jock didn't suffer fools gladly, but he was a tremendous one for bringing young people on. He just plucked them out of Scotland. They were electricians one week and playing in the First Division the next. Whether that was always to the benefit of the lads playing round them, I don't know, but I do know that Jock rated Gary very highly. I can't speak for Jock, but I'm sure he wouldn't mind me saying he thought Gary was absolutely terrific as a bloke, the way he maintained and handled himself, and as player as well.'

Wallington's own reservations about Lineker as a player did not prevent his offering the young newcomer whatever advice he could, or from socialising with him away from Filbert Street. 'We worked quite closely together in the early stages,' he says. 'I'd say to him, "Just hold, a keeper will always commit himself." Then I would say, "What would you do in this position? Keep hold of the ball here because the goalkeeper will always go down." I'm not saying for a minute that I taught him all he knew, but goalkeepers and centre-forwards can help each other a lot. I've always worked with centre-forwards and asked them what they would do in certain attacking situations. Gary was only 16 or 17 at the time and I was the club skipper and senior pro, so it was the least I could do to take him aside for some individual coaching. "You've come too close to me," I'd say. "You've got to push it wider, or hold up. As long as you can hold it and keep your bottle, the keeper'll go."

'Because we would work like this, we had a friendship outside football as well. I love cricket, and Gary, a useful batsman who kept wicket not badly, turned out once or twice for some of the teams I had. He also came and played for the team I used to play for, Egerton Park of Melton Mowbray. We had a lot of cricket matches during the summer of my testimonial year. Gary was always first on the list to play and to help. He was also very big friends with Willie Thorne, the snooker player, of course. And there was one occasion during my testimonial year when he helped set things up for me. I'd put my arm round him and said, "Come on, you can help me out on Saturday. You're doing bugger all: you're only down that bookie's and I don't want that. You can come and help me." We'd got this exhibition snooker match arranged with Willie up at Filbert Street and we had to carry the heavy slates for the snooker table up a flight of stairs. There are eight slates in the bed of a full-sized table, and they are really heavy, I can tell you. There was only Gary, myself and another lad, and we had to manhandle the slates up those stairs. But he was straight into it. Little did I realise I was getting him into training for carrying his wallet!'

Operating in tandem, Lineker and Alan Smith scored 112 goals between them for Leicester in the three seasons between 1982 and 1985 and developed an understanding they were never really able to recreate when they played together for England. But Wallington reckons there was no great mystery about the reasons for the success of the partnership. 'It was the old combination,' he says. 'You've got a lad who's a goalscorer – Gary, by that time, had learned that he'd got to be moving wide and drifting in and varying his runs – while Alan was a good, tall, steady lad, another one who developed as soon as he left Leicester. I think it was the perfect combination – a bit like Toshack and Keegan. You've got a target-man there who could get the deft flicks, and you've got a lad who was beginning to read the through ball – checking and changing within the area and becoming very dangerous. He's got a quick mind, you see: that's the beauty of Gary. You can get a lad with quick feet who's totally brain-dead; but if you've got a quick mind, it makes all the difference. The number of times you see Gary go to hit a ball, somebody's come across, he's checked, then just toe-poked it or lifted it. It looks like a mis-hit into the corner, but it's not. It's just that he's got the quickness of brain to adjust.'

The partnership between Lineker and Smith is remembered fondly by the man who created it, Gordon Milne. 'They were as raw as they come,' recalls the former Preston, Liverpool and England midfielder who managed Leicester between 1982 and 1986. 'Alan had come from non-League football. But I thought, "Christ, keep these two together for five years, and we'll have the perfect combination." Milne never saw that plan come to fruition because he was obliged to sell Lineker to Everton in 1985 and left Leicester himself the following year to manage abroad. In August 1992, he was entering his sixth year with Besiktas, Turkish champions for the previous three seasons. 'Gary and Alan were just beginning,' he added. 'They were both totally unassuming, and they just gelled. Alan knew Leicester as well as Gary did and had learned the game the hard way. It was just a lovely combination at that time for a team in the Second Division. Then we got out and managed to hang on in the First. But I was so pleased to see them both have the careers they have had.

'What delighted me in Gary's case was that he improved his game and realised the potential that was there. Success hasn't spoiled him, either: he's remained almost as he was. A lot of them change don't they? Mind you, there were days when he could be irritating. You'd think, "Bloody hell, Gary! Are you awake this morning or what?" But even if you tore him off a strip, it wouldn't make him bitter or anything. Similarly, if he'd scored three on a Saturday, he was no different on the Monday than if he'd had a stinker. He was just an easy-going lad. He was never treated at that time as though he was anything special, because he hadn't proved anything. He never looked at himself in that way, in any case. He was just this youngster with a tremendous ability to score goals, and very, very quick, who was going to be an interesting proposition. He was never an outgoing sort of lad, never arrogant or cocky. If there was a criticism of him when he was young, it was that he didn't truly believe what was happening to him. You wanted a bit more from him. But that comes with maturity and experience.'

While Milne corroborates to a large extent Wallington's account of Lineker's development at Filbert Street, he clearly had a higher opinion of the young striker. 'I think there was a period early on when I even left him out of the team!' he says. 'He was very much a boy then by comparison with what you've seen of him in the last two or three years. He was very raw, really, at that time. But you could see in him the quality that indicated he would score goals. You just had this feeling that he was a natural goalscorer. At that time, also, he went through a little period when he got colds, a bit of this, a bit of that, and got himself run down. In the first year we got out of the Second Division, he was probably not as strong physically as he later became. When the physical strength came, and the confidence that comes with it, it made him an even more exciting proposition.

'The other thing about him that stood out was that he was very much a home-loving boy and very family orientated – and his was a Leicester family. So he was very pro-Leicester. He'd always been a supporter: Keith Weller and Frank Worthington were the types he looked up to. That was the lovely thing about him – as a local lad, he probably knew more about the club and the team and the town than a lot of the other players who were coming and going on transfers. There was a time when, if there had been a little spark more at Leicester, a little bit more opportunity, some indication of really trying to do something, he might not have signed for Everton. Because he was a Leicester boy, through-and-through, there was always a little thought in the back of his mind that he might stay on for another year or so. But it was not to be. It was time for him to move – there was no question at all about it.'

Because Lineker had been in and out of the first team under Jock Wallace, Milne was probably the first to have to come to terms with Lineker's curiously detached attitude to the scoring of goals, an unusual quality not all of his managers have been able to handle with equanimity. 'He was a competitor,' says Milne, 'but when he missed a chance, it never bothered him. You wondered sometimes whether he felt things like other people. When he scored a goal, he enjoyed it; but he didn't go crazy about it. Sometimes, to be honest, he could be a bit matter-of-fact. But when he did pop up and score a goal from nothing, it wasn't a surprise. I think it was just that he knew his own capabilities, really. Regularly in a match he'd miss three or four clear-cut chances, then score a goal from nothing – score one he should never have scored. He let other people worry about his misses – mainly the manager.'

Lineker could also be infuriatingly casual in training, a characteristic he developed early and has continued to display in varying degrees throughout his career. 'He was never an arrogant person, or a difficult lad to handle,' says Milne, 'but – and I think he would admit this himself – he didn't enjoy doing a lot of tactical or technical work. He liked to do the things he enjoyed doing – shooting, twisting and turning and sprinting. He was never what you'd call lazy, but always in training there was a lot in reserve. I never used to do that much from a tactical point of view with him in a group, because you'd always have to push him. In the six-a-side games we had – speaking as an old midfield player myself – he was lovely to play with because every time you had the ball he was always looking for it behind people. So even in those games, where he probably wouldn't push himself flat out, I saw the characteristics in him that I was looking for on a Saturday. But if you were doing six laps or something, he'd probably come last. Different people have different ways, and Gary's attitude to training never bothered me.'

It did bother some of his Leicester team-mates, though, according to Wallington. 'You've got to admire the lad for saving his energies, if you like, for match-days,' says the former Leicester skipper. 'You get very good training-ground players and very good match-day players, and the two don't often go hand-in-hand. Gary's career has always been based on putting the ball in the net; and while he was doing it, terrific. You can't argue with that, although one or two of the other lads were very envious of him. There they would be flogging their guts out, running up and down, getting bollockings right, left and centre, and there's Gary just staying within the 18-yard box and going, "Thank you very much!" But there again, he was that quality of player you don't argue with.' Milne supports that view by adding, 'Gary would probably be one of those at the back of the pack when it came to jogging round and that sort of thing, but his team-mates knew what he could produce. You always had this feeling that, if you were in trouble at any stage, he could find a goal for you. In my time at Leicester, a lot of his goals were out of nothing – which can turn a game for you.'

One of the early faults that had to be ironed out of Lineker's game was an inability to play with his back to goal. 'That was something we had to work on,' says Milne. 'We used to hit a lot of stuff up to him and he wouldn't hold it up. He'd even go down: he was always on the bloody floor! The ball would bounce off and he'd be on his backside or his face.' Jon Holmes was so worried about this weakness in Lineker's game that he thought of getting some outside help. 'Gary used to fall down a lot,' he admits. 'His balance didn't appear to be very good. I had a chat with Shilts [Peter Shilton, the former England goalkeeper] about it and I thought about getting Gary to talk to Lenny Hepple [an expert on balance who helped several footballers] but didn't go through with it. Peter said if they fall down it's often a sign they are not that brave; but I said that wasn't true in Gary's case. I don't know what happened exactly, but the problem just seemed to disappear after a time. Whether he got stronger or whether he worked on it himself, it just seemed to improve. Whether it was a case of someone else saying something and him thinking about it and then correcting it, I don't know, but it disappeared. If Gary thinks about something, he can actually make progress. Maybe he just didn't consider he did fall over or hadn't thought about how to stop doing it. And once he'd thought about it, he was able to get out of it.'

Milne, who always believed that Lineker's strengths outweighed his weaknesses, reckons the player benefited from the change of tactics he introduced when he took over from Jock Wallace. Interestingly enough, in view of the tactical effect Lineker was to have on Everton and the controversy that attended his relationship with England manager Graham Taylor, Milne insists that Lineker was always happiest in a team playing good football.

'Jock was known for the fact that he didn't mess about with his game. He got the ball forward a lot and pushed on a wee bit. When I went to Leicester, I changed it. You don't know who to believe, but the story is that it suited Gary more than kicking the ball long.

The thing about it was that if you just hit it direct, he wouldn't get on to those. But when there was a build-up, he would lose people. He would drift into areas where he could get a little bit of freedom; and at the right time the pass was being delivered, he was in. Without question, that was one of his qualities. He had the brain to know when and where to go. He was looking for the ball early, but if the centre-half had it he wasn't interested. If it was knocked around a little bit, and the play was changed a wee bit, then he was the one who was looking.

'I always said that he was a midfield player's dream. If you were a passing midfield player, he was a dream to play with. I felt a lot of his runs were very intelligent in terms of where they started from. He'd come on the scene all of a sudden and it wasn't by chance. He did that little bit of a half-loop away and just waited and waited for the move to develop. Because of that he was always a threat, no matter how teams tried to defend against him. He was a wonderful weapon to have. He'd get you a goal out of nothing, and you could always throw the ball in behind defenders and he'd cause problems that way. I always felt a footballing team was better for him because they'd play to his strengths.'

Milne must have wondered, though, whether he had got it right when promoted Leicester lost six matches straight off on their return to the First Division in 1983–84. In fact, they lost eight and drew two of their first ten games. Yet Lineker still managed to score four goals in this disastrous spell, proving he was not merely a fair-weather striker. In all, that season, he got 22 League goals in 39 appearances. Smith weighed in with another 13 and, between them, they dragged Leicester up to the safety of fifteenth place. Lineker's reward was to be included in the England squad by Bobby Robson. He made his international début as a substitute against Scotland at Hampden Park on 26 May, 1984.

The following season, 1984–85, proved to be Lineker's last at Filbert Street. It was hardly surprising that other clubs should come flocking round, since he scored five goals in the club's opening six games and followed that with a number of outstanding perform-ances. Perhaps the best was at Queen's Park Rangers on 4 May, 1985. He scored two stunningly brilliant goals and made Leicester's other one in a 4–3 defeat. This time, his season's haul was 24 goals from 41 appearances and his partnership with Smith brought 36 goals. It was quite an eventful season, all-in-all. A hat-trick Lineker scored in a 6–1 third round FA Cup victory at Burton Albion was expunged from the record because a missile thrown from the crowd hit the Burton goalkeeper. A replay behind closed doors was ordered by the FA.

Other developments, too, were taking place out of sight of the public. 'We said, "All right, his contract is up – we'll wait and see what happens",' recalls Jon Holmes of that end-of-season period in 1985. 'There had been all sorts of rumours. Spurs were reckoned to be in for Gary, and Bari, the Italian club, came in. But I told him I didn't think he should be thinking about them at that stage. "If you go abroad," I said, "you go to a really big club." So we turned them down out of hand, but Paul Rideout and Gordon Cowans went. It was fair enough for them, and I've nothing against Bari, but I didn't think it was right for Gary at that time. Nothing much happened until his contract came to an end. Nobody was apparently in for him.

'Then I went off to play in a golf weekend. I drove all the way down to Sandwich, and when I arrived there was a call from Gary saying Everton had come in. And I thought, "Oh, bloody hell! I've only just got here." Anyway, in the end I said, "OK, I'll come up and meet them with you." So I drove all the way back up to the Coventry Post House and met them there. We fiddled about with the deal and I suggested they took a bit of time to think about it. So we got the bid and I drove back to Sandwich that night. I've never driven so far in one day: I'd just bought a Spandau Ballet tape, and it was on every time I got in the car. It must have played about 100 times, and in the end it drove me mad. I've not played it since!

'By the time I got back to Sandwich, it was said that Liverpool were in as well. Alan Bennett, the Leicester secretary, rang me half an hour later. We think Gordon Milne tipped them off. He's an ex-Liverpool player, of course. But Gary really wanted to move to Manchester United. When he was first out of contract, I had rung Ron Atkinson and said, "Look Gary's interested in coming to you. Are you interested?" "Very interested," he said. "If he wants to go anywhere else, he's mad. I'm going on holiday to Marbella. Let my chairman know if anything happens." So when I got back to Sandwich, I rang Martin Edwards, the Manchester United chairman, and he said, "Yeah, we'd better look at it, blah, blah, blah." Then he rang me back and said, "Listen, we can't flog Frank Stapleton, this, that and the other. We can't do the deal now."

'So there was only Liverpool and Everton. He'd never wanted to go to Anfield because he felt he couldn't play with Ian Rush. There was also this factor that Liverpool had always kept their players in the reserves for a year or so. It was the year before the 1986 World Cup, and somehow or other Gary knew this World Cup was going to be critical for him. Anyone who wanted to play at international level would have been thinking about the World Cup, of course, but it was interesting that he guessed that it would be his big moment – and of course it was.

'I'd had Howard Kendall going backwards and forwards, and the next night I rang Gary from Sandwich. I said, "In a sense he's right to push for a decision, and you don't want to go to Liverpool." "Well," said Gary, "Gordon Milne says I've got to talk to them." So I said, "If you don't want to talk to them, you don't have to talk to them. You're at the end of your contract. You can do what the hell you want. I think it's better not to talk to them just to say you are sorry." Gary's dad came on the 'phone and asked me what I thought. I said, "Well, Everton are offering quite a good financial deal, I think Kendall's right for him and they are a good club who have just won the championship." And he said, "Well, if you think it's all right, I think it's all right. Better leave it to Gary." Then Gary came on and said, "Yeah, let's go for that!" So I rang Howard and he was obviously delighted to get the good news.

'On the Saturday, I went back to Nottingham, Gary came up and we drove from there to Liverpool. We did the press conference, Gary had his medical and we signed the contract. Even at the age of 24, his sense of public relations was very good. He said, "Everton's always been my number one club." Which, strictly speaking, wasn't true; but it was the right thing to say in the circumstances. Actually, Everton probably were number one after Manchester United said they couldn't sign him.'

Gordon Milne tells the story rather differently, though only in the sense that Lineker's first transfer proved to be anything but a quick sale. The amazing thing now, in view of the fame he has acquired, was the reluctance of the leading clubs to take a chance on him, to back their judgment with hard cash. 'At the time,' Milne recalls, 'Liverpool came on to me – being ex-Liverpool myself – and asked the question that really mattered. They'd looked at him and so had Manchester United. But you could look at Gary in those days and think, "Well, you know, maybe he scores goals, but he hasn't got much more to go with it." I gave a very high recommendation to Bob Paisley and they looked and looked and never came back. Manchester United did the same. Everton may have tried to mess us about at the tribunal [their offer of £400,000 was £600,000 below Leicester's valuation], but at least Howard came in for Gary. Tottenham were another club who'd asked the question. It was like saying, "Look, I've seen him play 17 games for you and he's scored 14 goals, but I can't see what's in him." Those were the sort of statements made, I promise you. But you could go and see Gary and think, "Well, I saw nothing today." But maybe five minutes from the end, or with the last kick of the game, he could pinch a bloody goal for you! He'd score three in a game and be in and out of it. So he was difficult to read correctly at the time.

'The advantage I probably had over all the other people who worked with him was that I saw him at the beginning, when he was growing up and learning. You've got to be a bit more tolerant then with players. When he left Leicester, I think he needed to be in the company of better players, because that's how you learn. He needed to be with a club that hired a higher quality of player and could be in a position to win tournaments. So he was ready to go into the next stage of his learning process. If you look at his career, the one thing that stands out is that he has always seemed to make the right move at the right time. Whether it happened by chance or through careful planning doesn't really matter.'

· 4 ·

Everton – Annus Mirabilis?

It was July 1985, and the transfer tribunal had just decided that £800,000 was the fee Everton should pay Leicester City for their free-scoring striker, Gary Lineker, then aged 24. Gordon Milne, the Leicester manager, who had seen the player develop from a raw lad into a real prospect, could not resist one final word as his club bowed to economic necessity once more. 'You don't know how good he is!' he told Howard Kendall, the Everton manager, almost defiantly. It was a remark Kendall had reason to remember as Lineker wrote himself into the folklore of Goodison Park and helped to alter the club's style of play during the course of one eventful season.

'I've said that to two managers,' Milne recalls. 'One was Howard and the other was George Graham. I said it to George about Alan Smith. I said it to Howard because we had a bit of nonsense at the tribunal, and I'm just pleased I was right. It's easy now for everyone to be an expert and say what a good player Gary is. The fact was that, when he was younger, a lot of people had looked and never moved. The so-called experts perhaps made a mistake. Those that did take a chance have obviously got their reward for it.'

'I don't think you do know how good people are until you work with them,' Kendall admits now of the player who was then the most expensive Everton had ever bought. 'He came in here and didn't knock the door down saying "Well, I'm the record signing!" He just got on with his job, which he was good at. He quietly came in and immediately impressed everybody around him – which is your first job, really – and then went from there.' And how Lineker went! Carrying on where he had left off at Leicester and revelling in the opportunity to play with better players, the young striker scored 30 goals in 41 League games, five in the FA Cup and three in the Milk Cup (League Cup).

Those 38 goals constituted a demonstration of sustained excellence that gradually won over a knowledgeable, discerning crowd brought up on the exploits of legendary centre-forwards such as Dixie Dean, Tommy Lawton and Alex Young, and resentful of the unproven newcomer signed to replace Andy Gray, the fearless, extrovert Scottish international striker unexpectedly sold to Aston Villa after achieving folk-hero status while helping Everton to win the FA Cup in 1984 and the League Championship and the European Cup-Winners' Cup the following year. In other words, Lineker's first step up into the big-time was not exactly strewn with rose petals.

'At Everton, it came off very quickly,' says Jon Holmes. 'It might have taken time in the fans' eyes because Andy Gray was such a legend – in some ways, I don't think we appreciated how big the Andy Gray thing was – but Howard had told me, "Andy Gray's going to go because he's not actually doing it away from home. It's the right time for him to make a move." It impressed me that Howard was not content to bottle out of the situation, that he was prepared to take the hard decision.'

Something of a depression had settled on Goodison at that time as a result of the indefinite ban from European football imposed on English clubs following the part played by Liverpool fans, ironically enough, in the Heysel Stadium disaster a few months earlier. But for that terrible loss of life at the European Cup final, Everton would have gone into the 1985–86 season looking forward to competing in Europe's major club tournament for the first time in 15 years. It was a disappointment that drove Kendall abroad eventually, but his excellent, hard-working team nearly succeeded in offering him immediate consolation in the meantime.

The side into which Lineker slotted was as well-balanced and smooth-running as a Swiss watch. By 1985, Neville Southall, Kendall's first signing after he became Everton's manager in 1981, was well on the way to becoming Britain's finest goalkeeper. In front of the big Welshman, a back-four of Gary Stevens, Derek Mountfield, Kevin Ratcliffe and Pat van den Hauwe offered a combination of pace, strength, aggression and aerial power that not only provided Southall with considerable protection, but could make an attacking contribution as well. Then, in midfield, the creativity of Trevor Steven and Kevin Sheedy on the flanks was underpinned by the combative industry of Peter Reid and Paul Bracewell in between.

Up front, Lineker found the ideal foil in Graeme Sharp, the tall, dark Scottish international striker who had become part of the Goodison furniture since being bought for £120,000 from Dumbarton by Gordon Lee, Kendall's predecessor, five years previously. Sharp, who had to adjust to a succession of partners during his 12 seasons with Everton, clicked more readily with Lineker than with most. His unlikely partnership with Gray, a striker out of much the same physical mould, had brought him 21 goals the previous season, but he was only two short of that total playing alongside Lineker, a goalscorer as different from Gray as it is possible to imagine.

The season in question saw Everton, for the second time running under Kendall's inspired management, come within a whisker of winning both the League Championship and the FA Cup – English football's classic double. The previous season, Everton had won the title by a distance from Liverpool, but had lost the FA Cup final 1–0 to Manchester United. This time, they were to be pipped at the post in both competitions, Lineker's goals notwithstanding. But what made it much, much worse was the identity of the team who did the pipping.

Liverpool, Everton's close Merseyside neighbours and fierce rivals, came from behind with a devastating late run of 11 wins and one draw to snatch the title away from the holders by two points. As it turned out, Everton paid dearly for losing 1–0 at Oxford, Les Phillips scoring the winner in the last minute, at the end of April, 1986. It is a game Lineker remembers for a miss that still haunts him. 'I had a chance, one-on-one,' he recalls. 'The keeper actually made a good save, but if that had gone in, we'd have won the League, I think. I've had a few embarrassing misses in my career – in fact, I've missed loads of chances – but if I had to nominate one, it would be the one at Oxford because it was so important. I lost my lucky boots that night. I'd scored something like 20 goals in 20 games, then forgot to put them in the skip. So I had to wear some borrowed boots. When I got my boots back, I scored five goals in the last two games. They were falling apart, but I had them repaired and took them to the finals of the 1986 World Cup,' (where he finished as the tournament's top scorer with six goals).

Just a week after Liverpool had finished top of the old First Division by winning 1–0 at Chelsea with a goal from player-manager Kenny Dalglish, the Reds again got the better of the Blues at Wembley as well. Liverpool came from behind to win the FA Cup. Lineker did his bit by giving Everton a half-time lead, only to see Ian

Rush, with two more goals against his favourite opponents, and Craig Johnston carry Liverpool to victory in the last 23 minutes of the game. They were sickening blows that, even now, are painful for Kendall to recall. Thinking of the defeats at Oxford and Wembley, he says ruefully: 'We missed out on the double by just two games – it was that close!'

Lineker was as downcast as anyone at this turn of events. 'A huge disappointment at the time,' he has called the loss of his only real chance of winning a League Championship medal. But he is never down for long. 'You want everything, don't you? But it's not always possible, and I don't think I can complain too much about what's happened to me, to be honest.' At the time, Lineker did at least have the consolation of knowing he had proved himself at the very highest level of the domestic game. Any doubts about his ability to operate successfully under pressure were soon dispelled as he proceeded to find the net at the phenomenal rate of a goal every 1.36 games – his most prolific spell anywhere until he finished his League career in England with the remarkable flourish of 28 goals in 35 games for Tottenham Hotspur in the 1991–92 season.

This, too, at a time when he was just beginning to establish himself in the England team. Having played – and scored twice – against West Germany and the USA in a pre-World Cup tournament in Mexico City during the summer of 1985, while still a Leicester City player, Lineker kept his place for the next four internationals, against Romania, Turkey, Northern Ireland and Egypt, scoring a hat-trick against the Turks. He appeared in only one of England's next four games, but had clearly done enough to persuade Bobby Robson, then manager of the national team, to include him in his squad of 22 for the 1986 World Cup finals.

With club and country, Lineker's scoring continued to be largely the product of the explosive acceleration that had got him noticed at Leicester. It was the principal reason Kendall had been willing to pay £800,000 for him (a fee that shot up to just over £1 million when Leicester collected a £250,000 bonus for the player's quick transfer to Barcelona) and it proved to be the catalyst for an unscheduled change in Everton's style of play.

'I'd sold Andy Gray to Aston Villa, and I just felt we needed more pace in the side,' recalls Kendall, who returned to Goodison Park as manager in 1990 after spells with Athletic Bilbao and Manchester City. 'Andy had been a tremendous guy and had made a tremendous impact here, but I still felt we needed more pace.

41

Amazingly enough, the way that we scored the goals then changed. The season before, when that team won the championship for the first time, the goals had been spread around the team. We'd had people like Kevin Sheedy, Adrian Heath and Trevor Steven weighing in with double figures, plus about 14 from Derek Mountfield at the back.

'When Gary came into the side, we became more direct, played a long ball. He used to exploit the space we have in English football between a square back-four and the goalkeeper. He was absolutely brilliant with that – the ball over the top, the pace on to it and the deadly finish. Nobody could catch him. So it was a case of Gary's goals, and not many from the other players who'd scored previously. It did change our style a little, though not deliberately: it was just something that came about because of the players we had. With Sheedy's vision and Gary's pace, it was often a case of the two-pass goal: the goalkeeper to Sheedy, Sheedy over the top to Lineker, Lineker goal. A lot of people think that's the way the game should be played all the time, but it's not as easy as that.'

Graeme Sharp, too, is quick to recall the change of style. Sharp, renowned for his effectiveness in the air, found it as easy to combine with Lineker as with Gray, but for different reasons. 'The way we played changed a little bit when Gary was in the side,' says the player who joined several other ex-Evertonians at Oldham in 1991 after 12 seasons at Goodison. 'Andy and I had a good partnership as well, but when he was with us it was a more cultured build-up with more passes. Andy and I never had any great pace, so when Gary came in it was a long ball, with a flick-on by myself or Kevin Sheedy's exquisite left foot. Kevin was putting balls in for Gary to run on to: in the end, Gary said "Just put it over, and I'll get there." And he was proved right.'

Mark Wallington believes what happened at Goodison Park was simply an extension of developments at Filbert Street. 'I can quite believe Everton became something of a long-ball team with Gary in the side,' he says. 'His strength at that time was the ball over the top. It was only when he went abroad and started to come back and link up that he became more of an all-round player. He had to drop deep to lose markers, because they wouldn't follow. Then he would spin and turn and hit them from deep. Whereas in English soccer – and especially the Second Division – he'd make even his own full-backs and centre-halves look good. They'd just play the ball over the top and he'd get on to it. "What a cracking ball that was," people would say. But it was only Gary's pace that had made the pass into a good one.

'I would agree with Howard Kendall that the people who played with Gary tended to become very lazy. I tell you what – I've seen the lad set off on three runs and just get his breath back. Then the opposition have pushed up, another ball's gone over the top and the poor lad's just stood and looked around as if to say, "How the hell do you expect me to get on the end of that!"'

Between them, Lineker and Sharp scored 49 of Everton's 87 League goals that season. Yet their striking partnership came about almost by accident. 'At first,' Sharp explains, 'there were three of us vying for two positions. There was Gary, myself and Adrian Heath. The gaffer kept changing it week-in and week-out, so the three of us decided to have a talk with Howard. We told him we'd rather have a settled partnership. Fortunately for me, it was myself and Gary first, and it took off from there.

'He was a joy to play with. The understanding wasn't something we set out to work on: it just happened. Gary had great awareness and was definitely the best finisher I've ever played with. In fact, he was the best attacking partner of the 13 or 14 I had in my time with Everton. Most of his goals were scored from close in. You wouldn't expect him to bang one into the top corner from 30 yards, or anything, but give him a chance in the six-yard box and the ball was in the back of the net. The hat-trick he scored against Poland in the 1986 World Cup finals proved that.

'His pace was a great asset as well. When he first came in, he was very, very quick. He had big legs – sprinter's legs. One of his goals for Everton that stands out was against Luton in the FA Cup. It was at Goodison and we won 1–0. Gary scored brilliantly through his pace. He also started to get goals with his head. When he arrived at Goodison I don't think he'd scored with a header. But he got something like 10 that season. He didn't score at all in the first four or five games, though. His first goal came down at Tottenham, and he took off after that. Even when he wasn't scoring, he was never worried. He'd say one would come along sooner or later. He was very level-headed like that.'

However, Jon Holmes reckons Lineker was always better with his head than anyone realised. 'I remember Howard asking me how good Gary was in the air. I said, "He's better than you think!" Then Howard rang after six weeks of the season and said, "You're quite right. He is better than I thought, because he's scored eight goals –

seven of them headers." It's not true to say Gary hadn't scored with a header. He'd scored quite a few – more than people perceived him as having scored. Let's put it like that.'

One thing Sharp recalls with some amusement was the continued infrequency of Lineker's training stints, a characteristic developed at Leicester that was to become a standing joke with club and country as his career unfolded. 'He never used to train,' says the Scot with undisguised bafflement. 'Everybody used to walk in and Links would be in the bath. "Not training today?" someone would ask him. "No, the gaffer just told me to rest," he'd reply. He'd train on a Friday, and that was it. As you can imagine, he got quite a bit of stick over it from the rest of the lads.'

All was forgiven on match-days, of course. Lineker earned the right to some special treatment by putting the ball in the net regularly enough to earn everyone a succession of win bonuses. There was also boundless admiration for his technique. 'Willie Donachie, Oldham's coach, is a great admirer of Gary's,' reports Sharp. 'In training, he says to the lads, "Watch Gary Lineker. He's always aware and he's always trying to get that edge on defenders." Gary's very intelligent. At the end of the day, the game's all about goals, and he's scored them.'

Lineker's admirers would add perseverence and strength of character to his formidable list of assets. 'If Gary misses a couple of chances,' says Howard Kendall, 'he still goes into those areas where he's had his chances. Even if the ball doesn't come, he still goes there. Whereas other players let their heads go down and think it's not going to be their day, he keeps going right to the end. His goal-scoring record proves what a great player he is, and so does the way he conducts himself on the field. He takes the challenges and just shrugs them off.

'At first, when I signed him, I thought that was going to be a weakness. After the signing, Jon Holmes said to me: "By the way, you know about his disciplinary record, don't you?" "Hang on, hang on," I thought to myself, "I've signed somebody who's going to be suspended in the early part of the season!" But when I asked Jon what he was talking about, he replied: "He's never been booked!" Then, since there weren't many stitches in Gary's face and his nose was still straight, I began to wonder whether he wanted to show aggression, wanted to win badly enough. He does, but he doesn't show it like other players by aggression or by mouthing. He finds space in the area, that's what he does; and his timing is perfect.

'His work in the penalty area has to be his strength. Most of his goals have been scored there. To be honest, I don't think he's a brilliant player technically. He's not one of those strikers who picks the ball up, turns and goes past two or three defenders. Jimmy Greaves could do that, but it isn't Gary's game. He knows his limitations and he doesn't go looking for the ball like Greaves. He'll be the target, then he'll set things up; but he's relying on other players to create moves for him to finish off.'

Most football managers have an inbuilt reluctance to dwell too long on the virtues of one particular player, however talented. Anxious not to give the individual too great a sense of self-importance and wary of undermining team spirit, they go out of their way to spread the credit as widely as possible. Thus Kendall still falls easily into the habits of his profession even six or seven years after the event: 'Gary certainly got the service with us – especially from the likes of Sheedy, who could put the ball on a sixpence. When he made his timed runs, the ball would get there. All strikers rely on service, and when you think you've got Sheedy on one side and Trevor Steven on the other, plus Graeme Sharp taking the weight off you up front, you can't really help but impress if you've got any ability.'

The point is, of course, that the whole thing worked very well. So why, then, upset the applecart by selling Lineker to Barcelona only a year after he had arrived at Goodison Park? Everton did not actually win anything during the one season he spent with them, true enough, yet he scored enough goals and the team went close enough to the silverware to suggest that great things lay ahead. The answer, in the main, is that Everton could not resist the purchasing power and glamour of a wealthy Spanish club prepared to pay £2.2 million for the Merseysiders' leading scorer. But it was not quite as simple and straightforward as that. According to Kendall, a former Everton player steeped in the club's 'School of Science' traditions, stylistic considerations were also a factor in the transaction.

'On the one hand,' says the Everton manager, 'we had changed our style of play: on the other, how can you stop someone leaving when Barcelona are involved? Liverpool couldn't stop Ian Rush going abroad, and most other top-class English players have gone, haven't they? At the same time, I did honestly feel we could still go on and win the title by reverting to our previous way of playing. That, in fact, is what happened the following season, though I'm not trying to take anything away from Gary.' Despite his obvious reservations about the effect of Lineker's pace on Everton's style of play, however, Kendall regrets that the player did not rejoin his old club – as Ian Rush did Liverpool – when he decided to return to English football in 1989.

'I think it was unfortunate,' he says, 'because the fans felt they'd only had 12 months to see someone special. It was only half a season, really, since Gary wasn't accepted by the Everton crowd as a replacement for Andy Gray until the December. In other words, they didn't really begin to appreciate his contribution until halfway through the season. Not only that, but Gary came back from Spain an even better player: his first touch had improved in terms of retrieving the ball and he'd had to work out a way of playing against man-marking and the sweeper system.'

On Lineker's return to England, he chose to follow Terry Venables, his first manager at Barcelona, to Tottenham. Kendall had also moved on by then, and Jon Holmes defends the player against any suggestion of disloyalty to Everton by claiming that the Merseyside club's attempt to re-sign his client was little more than 'a gesture'. But we run ahead of ourselves. In May, 1986, the player was simply bemoaning his luck at having missed out on League Championship and FA Cup medals and listening to growing speculation about a transfer to Barcelona for a massive fee. He was also looking forward to playing for England in the finals of the World Cup the following month, an experience that was to change his life dramatically for the better.

Meanwhile, quite a lot was happening behind the scenes. 'At the end of that season, Everton played at Watford,' says Jon Holmes, taking up the story. 'It was a vital game which they won 2–0. Bobby Robson, the England manager at that time, was in the boardroom after the match and I'd been nattering on to him about Tony Woodcock because of the World Cup – as it happened, he left Tony out of the squad. Then Howard came in and Bobby started to talk to him. But I could see Howard making faces to me and letting me know he wanted a word. Eventually, he came over and said, "I'm glad you're here. How do you fancy going abroad? I've got to tell you Barcelona have been in. We've put them off, but they've come back. It's a lot of money and I feel I ought to offer Gary the chance to go or not. I'll put it to him tomorrow."

'That's what he did, so Gary rang me and we had a discussion. Howard had told me Juan Gaspart, the vice-president of Barcelona, was going to ring me, but he didn't. It was all on and off, on and off.

Gaspart was ringing and we were supposed to have a meeting, then nothing happened – typical Barcelona scenario. Then, when I'm on the same golf weekend at Sandwich as the previous year, Gaspart eventually rings me. "We want you to come out to Spain," he says. This was the day England played their second game of the 1986 World Cup finals – the one against Morocco, when Ray Wilkins got sent off. Gaspart wanted me to go out the following Thursday, the day after England were due to play Poland. So it was all set up: that was the day I would go.

'I was speaking to Gary in the meantime, but he's always been content to get on with what he's doing and leave it to me to sort things out. I've always told him exactly what's going on: I don't withhold things because I think that's immature. That's what drives me mad about football managers sometimes – the way they think they can flog players and conceal it. And they expect them to play for them even though they've been trying to flog them. When a footballer asks for a transfer, it's outrageous and they are trying to break their contract. When a club tries to sell a player, it's just normal business and accepted behaviour.

'Anyway, I kept Gary in touch with what was going on, and he obviously knew I was going out to Barcelona the day after the Poland game. So it's not really true to say it was that game [in which Lineker scored a famous hat-trick] that made the transfer, because it was already on. The only thing Gaspart said after it was, "Oh, it'll cost us more money now!" As I recall, it didn't cost them more because Everton didn't relent on their deal and I only knew of the money after the game.

'So then we went backwards and forwards and fiddled about. Eventually, Barcelona said I could sign for Gary and they would be happy with that. But I insisted we wait for Gary. They said they couldn't wait, so the family and I had a meeting on Gary's father-in-law's lawn. I said I could either take the contract out to Mexico or we could wait until the World Cup was all over. I told them that, personally, I'd rather wait, but that I couldn't take the responsibility myself. When I asked the family what they thought, they agreed that I should tell Barcelona to wait. So I did, and it was all tidied up when Gary came back from Mexico. There were doubts all the way, because I'd wanted him to think about it, and it was possible he would turn it down.'

While both Everton and Lineker did well out of the deal, it emerges now that the fee was actually quite a bit smaller than the one that has gone into the record books. 'I saw the contract,' says Holmes, 'and the fee was £2.2 million. Publicly, it varied between £2.75 and £2.8 million. I don't know why football clubs tell lies or why they allow lies to be perpetuated. They told me Ian Rush's fee was £2.8 million, but it wasn't cash. This was £2.2 million, and it was cash up front.' He is no less forthcoming, either, about Lineker's personal terms. 'People talk about a lot of money, but I don't know what they mean by that. It would have earned Gary over three times what he was getting at Everton, which is a lot of money. The way the money's gone in England the last few years, it probably doesn't sound so much now. But at that point – we're talking six years ago – it did seem a lot of money. He was earning over £250,000 a year at Barcelona and it was an eight-year contract. I think that was because, over there, at the end of the contract, you were always on a free transfer. That's why they make the contracts so long; but it was never expected to be seen out. We never really wanted it that long, but the club wanted six, so we thought we might as well have eight to give us some long-term security. If he was injured, the contract said, he got the money anyway. So it did give him a certain amount of security.'

· 5 ·

Barcelona – Heaven

Gary Lineker moved from Everton to Barcelona in a blaze of publicity during the summer of 1986. His six goals for England in the finals of that year's World Cup, coming on top of his 38 for Everton, had made him one of the hottest properties in world football, and his public profile has grown accordingly. Gary and his fiancée, Michelle Cockayne, had planned a quiet wedding in their home town of Leicester before moving to Catalonia, but they discovered to their surprise and dismay that 300 of their uninvited fellow-citizens wanted to be at the ceremony as well. The media crush alone was so great that the official photographer could not get through, a hitch that had the bride in tears. However, it was only a momentary show of disappointment by a petite, attractive young lady whose remarkable toughness, determination and strength of character have helped carry her and her husband through some of the sternest challenges they have faced. Events were to prove that Lineker had made a wise choice of partner for married life.

Barcelona and their vast stadium, the Nou Camp, are so different from Everton and Goodison Park – not to mention Leicester City and Filbert Street – that they might almost be on a different planet. The culture shock for anyone moving house from England to the Catalonian capital must be great. This Mediterranean coastal city and the surrounding region ache for freedom from Spain; they have a fortress mentality. The first instinct of the Catalonian is to look inwards, to glory in the achievements of his or her own people. Thus the importance of everything is heightened by a striving to be better at it than any of the so-called Spanish oppressors. And nothing represents that craving for superior self-expression more prominently than Barcelona Football Club.

Rob Hughes, the distinguished *Sunday Times* and *Herald*

Tribune sports writer, caught the flavour of the situation exactly and evocatively in *Golden Boot*, a biography of Gary Lineker published in 1987. 'The goalposts in Barcelona's awesome Nou Camp stadium are the same distance apart as in any other; all else is vastly out of proportion,' wrote Hughes. 'Barcelona is less a football club than a life force, an outlet for five million Catalans to express their separate ideals as opposed to Spanish rule from Madrid. Fail to grasp that and you fail to reach Barcelona's wavelength.

'The burden has broken some of the great names in soccer coaching: Italy's Helenio Herrera, Spanish-naturalized Hungarian Ladislao Kubala, Dutchman Rinus Michels, West Germans Hennes Weisweiler and Udo Lattek, Argentine Luis Cesar Menotti. "It's not a sane mentality here," articulated Michels, who took Holland to two World Cup finals. "Results are far too important. Barcelona is a club with 120,000 places but represents five million people. Historical, political and sporting grounds are interwoven: one man cannot change that."

'The task is not to change Barcelona but to live with it, succeed with it. There are great wells of disparate energies there, obscene wealth, constant seething internecine undercurrents. Enter with a sound heart, an instinct to know which current to swim with and watertight legal advice, and the opportunities for high profit and quick success are abundant.'

Those juicy prospects, and the challenge of succeeding abroad, had lured Terry Venables to the Nou Camp in the summer of 1984. But the former manager of Crystal Palace and Queen's Park Rangers was by no means an automatic choice as Barcelona's new coach when Luis Cesar Menotti decided the hot seat at the Nou Camp was no longer bearable. Venables's main rival for the vacancy was the Swiss-German, Helmut Benthaus, and both men were interviewed by the president of Barcelona, Jose Luis Nuñez and his senior vice-presidents.

When it came to a boardroom vote, there was strong support for Benthaus because he shared a common language with Bernd Schuster, the gifted German midfielder, whose importance to the club had increased with the imminence of a troubled Diego Maradona's departure from the Nou Camp. However, there is a long tradition in Spanish football of employing English coaches, and Nuñez's admiration for the British game was well known. The enormously wealthy and all-powerful Barcelona president had tried unsuccessfully to buy Liam Brady and engage Bobby Robson as coach, and he did not mean to fail again. Thus, Nuñez used his influence to bring about the appointment of Venables, then only 41 and virtually unknown in Spain.

The Englishman could scarcely have made a better start. Barcelona's first match of the 1984–85 season was away to Real Madrid, leading representatives of the Spanish domination so resented in Catalonia. There could not have been a bigger test for Venables, but his team carried him through it with a victory that quelled all doubts about the newcomer's credentials and established him immediately as a local hero. Barcelona did not look back from then on. They lost only two of their 34 games that season and finished 10 points clear of Atletico Madrid at the top of the Spanish League. It was the first time for 11 years that the Catalan club had won the title – since Johan Cruyff's days as a player with them, in fact – and Venables earned himself the right to do more or less as he pleased for a while.

The trouble is, he had given himself a hard act to follow. The following season, 1985–86, was not quite so successful. Although Barcelona finished second in the League, it was to the arch-enemy, Real Madrid, and a long way behind. Then having got within touching distance of his club's most cherished target, the European Cup, Venables's team lost on penalties to the rank outsiders Steau Bucharest in the final. Thus, as that summer approached, Venables – or El Tel, as he was known by now to the English tabloids – was beginning to think of injecting his team with some new attacking blood. Steve Archibald, the former Clyde, Aberdeen and Tottenham striker, had done an excellent job for Barcelona, but the prolific Scottish international was then approaching 30 and Venables had decided to replace him with England's rising star, Gary Lineker.

It was not a decision the then Barcelona coach took lightly, as he explains. 'There's no secret why I bought Gary Lineker: he scores goals. I had to find somebody to follow Steve Archibald, one of the best strikers I've worked with. He was a very underrated player – great to work with and quite challenging. I'd heard he didn't like working hard, he didn't like coaching, but I found him just the opposite. When I was at QPR and we played Tottenham, every time Archie had the ball you felt he was going to hurt you. When I went to Barcelona, Maradona had to go. He had a financial problem and was in bad shape [plus ça change?]. We got £6 million for him and I had to find a replacement. Barcelona wanted me to buy Hugo

51

Sanchez (Real Madrid's Mexican international striker), and he looked a good player when I watched him. But I knew Archibald and I felt comfortable with him. As it turns out, Barcelona's suggestion would have been a good one anyway, but I had to win that argument because they are like bullies there – they want to choose everyone.

'It turned out Archie was good for me, because we won the League. He really was a super front player. But then I had to find another one. I met Gary and it was his intelligence that was important. You knew he would settle down in Barcelona like Archibald did, and you knew he would pick up things like Archibald: he would be interested. He had his own devices, anyway. I'm not saying I added much to that, but if you wanted him to do something he would soon pick it up. His runs became better, for instance.

'There's a lot of things he can't do – his heading ability is only adequate – but he's got intelligence. What I like about Gary is that he's got it all worked out. He likes it when it's all worked out and he knows what he's supposed to be doing as a footballer. So you want to choose him. The man is very intelligent and he's got a good agent in Jon Holmes, who's also very intelligent. The two of them together, I think, wouldn't make too many mistakes.'

As Venables suspected, Lineker settled down quickly in Barcelona and positively revelled in his new Mediterranean lifestyle. He and Michelle set up home in a luxurious, four-bedroomed villa on an exclusive estate, Sant Just Desvern, about five minutes drive from the Nou Camp. It was one of those walled estates for which a pass is needed to gain entry, and they had use of a communal swimming-pool and communal tennis-courts, all fringed with palm trees. Both Gary and Michelle loved the warm climate, dined regularly at Barcelona's famous seafood restaurants and became friends with two of Spain's leading opera singers, Jose Carreras and Monserrat Caballé, as well as Ms Caballé's niece, as they widened their cultural interests. Crucially, they also wasted no time in learning the language.

'Michelle actually put the half-nelson on Gary and made sure he went to Spanish classes right from the start,' says Graham Turner, an English sports writer based in Spain, who acted as Venables's interpreter throughout his three and a half years at the Nou Camp and as friend and confidant to the Linekers and Mark Hughes as well. 'Michelle was very supportive,' adds Turner, 'and Gary made the effort. As a result, they both became fluent Spanish speakers. In fact, Gary still does interviews in Spanish when required.'

Brandishing a whip behind them both, as it were, was Jon Holmes. Drawing on the experience of one of his own clients, Tony Woodcock, and deducing from general observation that the British footballers who did best abroad were those who took the trouble to learn the language, Lineker's agent laid down the law. 'I said he'd got to learn Spanish and, to be fair, he took that on board. I said: "Look, Tony Woodcock's been to Germany. He worked hard to learn the language and get them on his side. You've got to do the same if you are going to go to Barcelona." And he did: he set to it. Fortunately, Michelle was keen on it as well, so they helped each other. Now, it's arguable which of them's better at Spanish. They are both very good.'

Lineker's realisation that he had to adapt as quickly as possible to the Spanish way of life, and the sense of well-being that brought in its wake, was reflected in his play. Despite the technical and tactical adjustments necessitated by the switch from English to Spanish football, he continued to score at the rate of a goal every two games. His League record that first season at Barcelona, when his new club again finished second to Real Madrid, was 21 goals in 41 matches, including a tremendous hat-trick against the champions. But Lineker's pleasure at his own successful adaptation was tempered by the struggle Mark Hughes was having to come to terms with the demands of Spanish football and Spanish life.

Signed from Manchester United for £1.7 million a month before Barcelona bought Lineker from Everton for £2.2 million, the young Welsh international was like a fish out of water. On the field, for a variety of reasons, Hughes wasn't scoring goals or playing well: off it, a shy, lonely bachelor of 22, he was further isolated by his reluctance to learn Spanish. 'While the Linekers were attending Spanish classes regularly,' recalls Graham Turner, 'Mark, who lived on his own, just sort of nodded off in the afternoon and didn't turn up. Not being able to speak the language was one of Sparky's [Hughes's] problems. He needed someone to make sure he went to classes. When he went on loan to Bayern Munich, it was actually written into his contract that he would have to attend German classes.'

To their everlasting credit, the Linekers did everything in their power to help Hughes through his torment. Gary, 26 by then, protected his team-mate as much as he could in the Spanish press, and he and Michelle invited Mark round to their home as often as possible for meals. But nothing worked. 'It got to the stage,' says

Graham Turner, 'where Mark felt very awkward about playing gooseberry all the time. You have to remember that Gary and Michelle had only been married a few months and Mark began to feel he was intruding on their privacy.'

However, Terry Venables believes Hughes's reaction to that situation was simply a symptom of a deeper insecurity.

'Football is such an insecure life,' he philosophises, 'that your whole world relies upon how you are performing on the field. If things are going badly for you, you can't even cough right. So far as Mark was concerned back in 1986, he would have thought he was in the way at the Linekers' house because he had a real downer on himself at the time. I would think going to Munich, and then back to Manchester United (which is what happened to the Welshman over the course of the next two years), was a big weight off his shoulders.

'He and Gary were two different animals socially. But Gary was very good to Mark: in fact, they were good to each other. They were very friendly. Mark was perhaps a bit too young at the time to try his luck abroad. Two years later, perhaps, he might have coped better. Once you get people against you, as happened to Mark at Barcelona, it's very difficult to get them back again. That's when you've got to cut your losses and move somewhere else. Gary, on the other hand, loved it from the word go. So did his wife. The challenge of the language, the different way of life – you could see he fitted in straight away. Mark, though, was a bit outside of what he enjoyed. He wanted to be with his pals and have a few pints. By the time his girlfriend came out, a lot of the damage was done. But he and Gary were two great boys, and I liked them very much.'

What no-one anticipated was the difficulty Hughes would have in playing his normal game in Spanish football. His strength as a striker is his physical power and aggression, but Spanish referees are not as tolerant of that he-man style as their English counterparts. 'The problem Mark did have,' says Venables, 'was that a lot of the things he got away with in England were really frowned upon in Spain. All of a sudden, that part of his game was taken away and it was so frustrating for him. Every time he challenged hard for the ball, he got blown up by the referee. Everyone was getting angry and he wasn't scoring. Basically, it wasn't his fault – he'd gone from one type of game to another. Gary came from the same game, but had a different attitude to it. His game never relied on the physical confrontation that Mark was successful at.'

Hughes suggested in his autobiography that his lack of success in Spain could be attributed to his unselfishness: that he spent too much time trying to bring other players into the game when he might have been better off concentrating on trying to score himself. But that sounds a bit like rationalising an uncomfortable experience to make the memory of it less painful.

The player was probably being more honest with himself when he was quoted as saying: 'I tried to get the better of them physically, which was probably the wrong way to go about it, whereas Gary would try to do it with a bit of guile.' Whatever the reasons, Hughes did not last the course. By March 1987, he was out of the Barcelona first team, dropped for good following an embarrassing and costly dismissal from the UEFA Cup. Drawing 1–1 on aggregate with Dundee United in the second leg of their quarter final, Barcelona conceded two goals in the last five minutes at the Nou Camp.

Ironically, Hughes's place was taken by Archibald, the player Lineker had been bought to replace. For the Scot had not been sold, just mothballed for most of the season, following the arrival of the two other expensive British imports. There was a further blow for the Welshman at the start of the following season, when he became de-registered as a Barcelona player. Forced to choose between Hughes and Bernd Schuster, because the Spanish FA had gone back on a proposal to increase the number of permitted foreigners per club from three to four, Venables chose the German international midfielder. Thus, Hughes had little alternative but to accept the offer of a loan period at Bayern Munich, and he left for Germany towards the end of 1987.

Although many observers feel Venables introduced Spanish football to the typically English 'pressing' game – a style copied with great success by Arrigo Sacchi at Milan – the Londoner insists that his purchase of three British strikers should not be construed in any way as a deliberate attempt on his part to anglicise Barcelona's style of play.

'I wanted a man in the box who was going to score goals, and who could do it at the highest level in front of 120,000 people,' he explains. 'It was not necessarily because Lineker and Hughes were British that I signed them, but because I knew them. I felt comfortable with them. I can't see anything wrong with a manager who goes from Bury to Burnley and buys a Bury player. It's not because he wants to go out dancing or on holiday with them, it's because he knows what he's going to get. It's a case of better the devil you know. Sometimes, you buy someone fresh you think is good, and he shocks the life out of you. You've done your money, you're on a loser and you are on the way down. Feeling comfortable is a good basis for starting off, I think.

'There was no attempt to impose a British style of play on Barcelona. The trick was to combine the Spanish and English styles, because they've both got something to give. It's not a case of one or the other, it's a case of trying to make sure you get the best. The British have mental toughness in certain areas of the field, and are good at scoring goals.'

Lineker was certainly doing that, and improving his game at the same time. 'I think Gary,' says Venables, 'got to grips with the sweeper system and realised that his type of game was difficult to handle by a flat back-four or a sweeper. It speaks volumes for him.'

If any period in Lineker's career demonstrated beyond doubt what a good learner he is, it was those first couple of seasons at Barcelona. 'The best I've seen at attacking space,' Gary said, 'was Hugo Sanchez. I learned a lot from watching him. He scores an extraordinary amount of goals from corners, and my ratio increased enormously after studying exactly what he did. It's just movement basically. You make one run for the defender and one for yourself. Don Howe [the former England coach] used to say that, and he was exactly right. It's about checking to go one way, then just moving back. Hugo does that well. I don't want to give too many secrets away, but you don't even have to sprint. It's just a question of backing off while defenders are ball-watching.

'I think you pick up bits from all the great strikers. Careca [Brazil] and Völler [Germany] for example are two great goalscorers without doubt. You've got to see players a lot to learn anything from them, and Real Madrid were on TV every week when I was in Spain. Every time we weren't playing, they were on the box and Hugo Sanchez scored a hell of a lot of goals. He was a great player and, at 34, still a very fit and agile man.'

What Lineker learned from Sanchez, he put to devastating use thereafter for club and country. But what makes Lineker really different from most other strikers, from most other British footballers in fact, is his ability to analyse and articulate how he does what he does well. 'I think nearly all my goals have been scored from around the six-yard box,' he said. 'I think I know basically what I'm doing in those circumstances and where I'm going.

'Nearly all my goals come from getting into areas where there are no bodies – taking chances, if you like. Attacking space is the secret. The largest percentage of my goals are scored like that. I can only remember one that I've hit from 25 yards into the top corner. That was against Manchester United a couple of years ago. It gave me enormous pleasure because it was always one of my ambitions to score a goal like that. Mind you, the chip with my left foot against Northern Ireland was probably the best goal technically I've scored for England.

'At all levels, you've got to take a chance and attack space if you are going to score a lot of goals. If there's a cross coming in and you are waiting to see where the ball's going to go, that's exactly what the defender does. In most cases, defenders are bigger and stronger than you and will win the headers. Even if you do win it, you are under pressure without getting a clear shot or header at goal. But if you attack space, by which I mean an area around the near post or the far post, before the ball's been crossed, that will give you a yard on the defender. Now, nine times out of 10 the cross will go no-where near you. But on the one occasion that it does, it means you'll probably have a clear chance three yards from goal. That's how you score goals.

'Barcelona is probably where I started working it all out – the why and the how. I think most of my goals in England before that were down to my pace. I used to score a lot of one-on-ones. But over in Spain – and the same applies in international football – when you've got man-for-man marking and sweepers, you can't score goals like that. So most of your runs have to be out wide. When the ball comes into the box, you have to attack space. I started working out how to get a different sort of goal from the ones I'd been getting before.'

Wherever football is played, though, the basics remain the same. Gary Lineker has scored goals everywhere not only because he was quick to learn and adapt, but because he has mastered the funda-mentals of attacking play. 'Very rarely does Gary shoot the ball over the bar,' Venables points out. 'OK, we can all remember the odd occasion when he's done it – like against the Republic of Ire-land in the 1988 European Championship – but usually he'll hit the ball low and make the goalkeeper work. You get so many people blasting the ball over the bar, but he just wants it on target. He knows that, with everything low, there is something possible for him.

'Two great strikers I've worked with are complete opposites –

Gary and Clive Allen. Clive is a great finisher and he will practise finishing. He didn't have pace, but he did have good, clinical finishing. I suspect Gary didn't like finishing exercises because he wasn't particularly good at them. But in the big moment, when it was important, his head was so good. Even when he was going, say, 10 games without a goal, his head was good. He knows it will come and he's not going to panic himself into losing possibilities.

'He's got the most out of himself as a footballer with his runs and the way he deceives defenders. His control is not great, but he gets himself into positions where he takes the pressure off his control. He doesn't always go flat, so that he's got to do something brilliant to get out of it. He gets himself on angles. He's learned that.'

Venables underlines his point by making a comparison between Lineker and Jimmy Greaves, the man generally regarded as the other great English goalscorer of the post-war era. It embarrasses Lineker to be compared with such great players because, no question of false modesty, he genuinely does not believe he is in their class. Nevertheless Venables, who was a team-mate of Greaves at Chelsea and Tottenham, says, 'The most important difference between them is that Gary knows what his game is, what he's got to do when he's outside the box and when he's inside it. I think Jim just played off the top of his head. He'd beat people with the ball – four or five of them. Gary wouldn't do that. It would be at the final moment, bump, and he would knock it in the net.

'Although Jimmy, skill-wise, was much better than Gary, Gary scored goals against the hardest opposition – the Chiles, the Argentinas and the like. If you look back, I think you'll find Jim was short with that. He'd score his four and five goals against Wales and Switzerland, and that type of opposition. On his day, though, Jimmy Greaves could be wonderful. He conjured up magic, like Maradona. But you end up saying you can't take it away from Gary because he did it in the biggest arenas and the most important matches, which I don't think Jimmy did. Gary had terrific pace and anticipation – he knew what he was about before the ball was kicked. That was the important thing about Gary – it was all between the ears with him.'

The drawback for a specialist goalscorer like Lineker is that he must keep scoring because he has very little else to offer. Once he stops finding the target on a regular basis he, like the gunslingers of the Wild West, is dead. Recognising this hard fact of life as a professional footballer, Venables says: 'The problem he's got is that as soon as he's not banging the ball in the net, the other players are not happy. And you cannot guarantee to people that you are going to score goals. But he's done it with such regularity that you've got to say, OK, he's not always going to score, but over the season he does win us a lot of games. It must be a strain to keep scoring like that all the time, but if there's one man who can cope, it's Gary Lineker.'

While admitting once that it did give him a great buzz to be England's number one striker, Lineker confessed that it had not been easy to maintain that lofty status. 'I set high standards,' he said, 'and it's always been difficult to live up to them. The higher you set them, the more demanding and difficult it is – because the moment you slip slightly the criticism starts, even though those stndards may be pretty good for others. That was the hardest thing I found about being successful at the top level. All of a sudden, if I went one or two games without a goal, I was under pressure for my place and I wasn't what I was. That was the one thing I found difficult to cope with, but fortunately I managed to keep knocking them in and, hopefully, will continue to do so.

'Individuals can either handle pressure or they can't. I don't think you can teach somebody how to handle the pressure that is undeniably there at the top level, especially in the big time. There's enormous pressure from outside and also from within. It's something you have to come to terms with yourself. Some do, some don't. It's the same thing when players look brilliant at a smaller club, get to a big club and never do anything.'

The obvious rapport between Venables and Lineker was rudely interrupted early in the 1987–88 season. Three defeats – two of them at home – in Barcelona's opening four matches put Venables's position in jeopardy. He jokes about it now with Graham Turner, but he was back in London on a short visit when he saw his journalist friend and interpreter in a television interview from Spain saying he thought Venables was likely to be sacked by the Catalan club. On his return to Barcelona, the Englishman discovered that everything had, indeed, turned sour and he left the Nou Camp near the end of September, 1987, in what Turner describes as 'half a sacking, half a resignation'.

Venables was succeeded immediately by Luis Aragones, the former Spanish international, former Real Madrid and Atletico Madrid player and former Atletico Madrid coach. He stayed for the rest of the season and steadied the ship sufficiently for Barcelona to win the Spanish Cup, beating John Toshack's Real Sociedad 1–0 in the final, and finish sixth in the League despite that inauspicious start. Nevertheless, it was still a fairly undistinguished season by their own high standards. So the 17 goals Lineker contributed in 36 League matches, plus four more in the Spanish Cup and UEFA Cup, were a measure of his ability to keep scoring in unfavourable circumstances.

No doubt it helped that he did not find it too difficult to strike up an understanding with the new coach. 'With Barcelona,' says Jon Holmes, 'it went very well for a year. The second was not quite so brilliant because Terry had left. Gary had his problems with Aragones to begin with, but then he got on well with him. Actually, the second season went quite well, because they won the Spanish Cup.' And that, of course, was the first major honour (discounting his Second Division championship medal with Leicester in 1979–80) Lineker had collected in a career which, strangely, turned out to be only moderately rewarding in terms of silverware.

There was a winners' medal to come in the European Cup-Winners' Cup the following season, but that had to be paid for in professional blood, so to speak, as we shall discover. Venables, meanwhile, was making his way to Tottenham, where Lineker would join him eventually. But neither man has ever quite severed the emotional link he established with the Catalonian capital. Both are welcomed warmly whenever they return, as when Venables was signing Lineker for Tottenham in 1989 and when Lineker was a member of the BBC TV commentary team covering the 1992 Olympic Games, the apotheosis of Barcelona as a city apart.

· 6 ·

Barcelona – Hell

1988 is not a year that Gary Lineker will remember with any great affection. For the first time in what seemed a charmed career, things started to go wrong that summer. The change began with England's poor showing in the finals of the European Championship and ended, the following summer, with Lineker's departure from Barcelona. In between, the player discovered he had been coming down with that most debilitating of illnesses, hepatitis, while playing for his country in West Germany. But perhaps an even greater scourge for him was the arrival of Johan Cruyff, the world-famous former Dutch international, as manager of Barcelona.

Cruyff succeeded Luis Aragones in the summer of 1988 and made it abundantly clear, as soon as Lineker had recovered from hepatitis in the autumn, that he did not have what you might call a particularly high opinion of the England striker. The prickly, strong-willed, opinionated Dutchman demonstrated what he thought of Lineker's ability by switching him from centre-forward to the wing, and by substituting him with monotonous regularity.

Cruyff brought off Lineker 16 times altogether that season, 1988–89. He also sent him on once as a substitute. This meant there were only 12 full matches among the 29 League appearances the Englishman made for the Catalan club during that particular campaign. Needless to say, his scoring record suffered accordingly. Only six goals – the leanest return since his early days at Leicester – were credited to his name. He did make up for it to some extent by claiming four goals in eight matches as Barcelona won the European Cup-Winners' Cup, but the writing was on the wall for him at the Nou Camp, and he knew it.

There was also a lot of writing about him in the newspapers as he and Cruyff slugged it out through the media. 'Everybody knows I'm a centre-forward, and I suppose Johan Cruyff knows it as well,' the player was quoted as saying, a mite sarcastically one senses. 'Well, he played against Lech Poznan as a centre-forward, so I think his comment is a bit stupid,' countered Cruyff sharply. In point of fact, Lineker had played only part of that Cup-Winners' Cup match at centre-forward: Cruyff switched him first to outside-right, then to outside-left.

'If Lineker does not understand my way of thinking, he can come and see me and we'll talk things over,' added the Dutchman in what seemed a conciliatory tone. But if the olive branch was being extended, it was dashed from his hand by the concurrent appearance in the best-selling British tabloid daily newspaper, the *Sun*, of an article headed, 'Lineker – The Big-Headed Flop'. Supplied by a French news agency, the piece quoted Cruyff as saying that Lineker was big-headed and unprofessional. But, ten days later, the paper had to issue an abject apology when it discovered the remarks had been wrongly attributed to the Barcelona manager.

Even so, the episode did nothing to improve the rapidly deteriorating relationship between Lineker and Cruyff. A note of desperation was beginning to creep into the player's public statements, as can be seen from the following: 'I'm not sure I've got the complete confidence of the manager. I'm not a winger and never have been, and I'm finding it very difficult to perform well.' Though not strictly true – in that Lineker had played on the wing many times for Leicester in the early days – the quote gives a fair indication of the state of mind that drove him, a man synonymous with the concept of fair play, to attempt to remove the number seven – the one Cruyff had condemned him to wear on his shirt – from the cards Barcelona held up to signal a substitution. Circumstances saved Lineker from uncharacteristic sharp practice, since the cards were stapled together and he could not wrench the seven out of the pack.

The reasons Cruyff gave for substituting Lineker so often were sometimes so cryptic as to be almost incomprehensible. 'I never change a player who's playing badly,' he said on one occasion. 'Basically, you cannot attack unless you dominate the match. I tend to sacrifice the player who defends the least.' There was no lack of clarity, however, about the interview the Barcelona manager gave to the Spanish weekly football magazine, *Don Balon*. Cruyff spelled out exactly why he was mistreating his English striker when he said, 'How many goals did Lineker score at centre-forward? Where does

Lineker fit into this team? Tell me how many goals he's scored, and then we'll talk about Lineker. [Marco] Van Basten [the Dutch international striker] would score 15 and set up 15 for his team-mates. It's better to change one player than to change the whole system. Lineker is a good player, but we simply play a different style. In England, he did well because systems are made to measure for his type of play.' Ironically, that was a policy statement which was to find an echo some four years later in the conflict between Lineker and the England manager, Graham Taylor.

At Barcelona in 1988–89, the player felt he was in a chicken-and-egg situation. Being shunted out to the wing reduced his chances of scoring goals: yet a lack of goals was being used as an excuse for excluding him from the team. But *in extremis* then, as in 1992, Lineker was not without support. *El Mundo Deportivo*, one of the two Barcelona sports dailies, who had headlined a November article about the player's problems, 'Lineker Like A Dizzy Duck', conducted a poll among its readers in December, 1988. The results showed that 69 per cent of the people consulted wanted the English striker to stay with the club. Lineker's natural aptitude for public relations stood him in very good stead during this difficult period of his life.

'You couldn't say Gary deliberately ran some kind of campaign,' says Graham Turner. 'It was just that he'd been a nice bloke to the media before Cruyff arrived, and he was a nice bloke after Cruyff was there. On top of that, Cruyff was not always coherent: he couldn't produce any real reasons for his treatment of Lineker. The man he played at centre-forward while Gary went out to the wing was Julio Salinas, who [at the time of writing] is still at the club though not a regular first-teamer. As soon as Gary left in the summer of '89, Salinas was then played on the wing.'

The biggest insult Lineker had to suffer from Cruyff during that turbulent season came on the day Barcelona played Real Madrid, symbol of the Spanish domination from which Catalonia would dearly like to escape, at the Nou Camp. This, of course, is Barça's most important fixture of the season and one which no player worth his salt wants to miss. Bobby Robson, then manager of England, was so sure Lineker would play that he took the trouble to travel to Barcelona to run the rule over his main striker. It proved to be a wasted journey, however. Cruyff had just signed a Paraguayan striker, Julio Cesar Romero, otherwise known as 'Romerito', and made sure he played. Having just stepped off the 'plane from South

America on the Thursday, 'Romerito' was rushed straight into the team to play Real Madrid on the Saturday. So Lineker, who had always scored goals against the old enemy, was left on the sidelines once more.

For the first time in his life, the lad from Leicester felt unwanted – and it showed. 'If I suspect for one minute any doubts on Barcelona's part, I won't tolerate it,' he said. 'For me, it has to be all or nothing. I would rebel against the prospect of being left to rot on the sidelines for a year. The money is good for the bank balance, but I couldn't afford to let that happen to my career. I would have to move on and I would be prepared to force the transfer. Everybody has known the side has not been playing well, but I don't think that was my fault. I think people realise it was not my fault if I was being played out of position. But I've never questioned the right of the manager to pick the team or field players in different positions.'

At least he could always turn to Jon Holmes for reassurance. 'We talked it out,' says the player's agent. 'It was hard for him, but he took it as a challenge. He felt he had something to prove and was going to prove it. I think that if he'd not been playing for England at the time, it would have been more difficult for him. It also helped that he had a lot of the press on his side. He quite enjoyed getting the Barcelona journalists on his side against Cruyff. There's no doubt he's got a natural gift for that. There was a lot of public interest in him, and I don't think the situation worried him too much because he knew he'd got a way out. I always told him there was no problem because there were plenty of clubs after him.'

What neither Lineker nor Holmes knew at the time was that Barcelona had approached Graham Turner secretly for help in selling the player. 'Barcelona contacted me to see if I could find Gary a club,' Turner reveals. 'They knew if I did the negotiating and it came to light, they could always say, "Oh, he's only a journalist!" I spoke to Alex Ferguson [the manager of Manchester United] and got myself involved in one of those coincidences you couldn't organise if you tried. Having asked me for the weekend to think about the deal and sort out the finance, Alex was back within quarter of an hour saying Cruyff had been on the 'phone with the same offer. So while the Barcelona board was trying to arrange the transaction discreetly and at several places removed from the club, Cruyff was obviously 'phoning round offering Lineker for sale.

'Eventually, it got to the stage where I couldn't keep it from Gary any more. It was a very uncomfortable position for me, especially when Alex Ferguson was about to have a word with Gary. At that juncture, it became pointless not bringing Gary into the picture. It became impossible to lie. It's one thing not to say something to people, but quite another to start lying to them. It then became a secret between Gary, Jon Holmes and me. And, of course, I mentioned it to Terry Venables: that's how the Tottenham connection eventually emerged. Terry and I are in touch all the time. He'd only been gone a year from Barcelona, so we were talking regularly.'

Meanwhile, Cruyff was strenuously denying all rumours that he was about to unload Lineker. 'I have not tried to sell Gary Lineker, and I have not spoken with anybody,' he told a press conference without any apparent embarrassment. 'If an offer is made, we will study it; but he is still a Barcelona player. I can understand that he is upset, because he has a reputation as a player who scores goals. But, at the moment, he is not doing it. I've always said that a player needs six to nine months to get over hepatitis, and I don't feel he is back to full fitness yet. He is a lovely lad and his behaviour is impeccable, but I'm not saying he is not transferable. If sometimes I feel I do not need Gary Lineker on the pitch, it is because I don't think he is at peak form. I feel he's lost the last half-metre, which makes the difference between being at 100 per cent and 90 per cent, between getting to the ball first or not. These sort of rumours are normal among people who are outside the club. The press have created the problem.

'I 'phoned Alex Ferguson, that's true. But it was not to sell Gary Lineker; it was to tell him that things which were being said were not true. People have come here in the name of Manchester United, so I 'phoned Alex Ferguson to ask him whether these two or three persons really had the authorisation to negotiate for the club, and he told me "no". We have not offered Gary Lineker to anybody. So there is no case to answer.'

Jon Holmes takes up this everyday story of European footballing folk by saying: 'It was obvious something was going to happen towards the end of that season, because Cruyff had tried to sell him. There were all sorts of rumours going about and, in the end, we got Barcelona to admit Gary could go. We said, 'Fair, enough; but it's got to be where we want to move to.' They said they understood that, and lined up all sorts of clubs, all sorts of deals. But all the time I kept knocking them down to try and keep the fee low; because the higher the fee the less there is in it for the player. Eventually, we reached a situation where Barcelona thought there were no clubs bidding at all: the clubs that were bidding I was telling not to bid in an attempt to keep the price down.

'We talked to Genoa, Monaco and Fiorentina. We also had PSV Eindhoven on the 'phone, and there was a bit of interest from Bayern Munich, plus loads of clubs from England. Queen's Park Rangers and Everton were two of them. I'd spoken to Jim Greenwood (the Everton secretary) and told him we had taken the decision that Gary didn't want to go back to Goodison Park. When the transfer to Spurs looked like going through, Jim rang me up and siad, "We are going to take some stick over this!" But I repeated that Gary had decided he wasn't going back, and that's that. Everton never really came rushing in. They had not made what you'd call a concrete offer largely because I'd led them to believe the transfer wasn't on.

'The Italians were quite interested, and we were interested in Fiorentina for some time; but then the coach, Sven-Goran Eriksson, went, and he was the bloke we thought really wanted Gary. They messed about, did Fiorentina. The financial offer they made was poor, and we went off them. Genoa were a promoted club at that time and we didn't know much about them. Gary met the coach and thought he was a complete bullshitter. The goalkeeper wasn't Shilton, but like Shilton; the number 10 wasn't Maradona, but like Maradona. It was the best team in the world according to him, but it was just ridiculous. Genoa did quite well, though, to be fair. They could have been a move for Gary if they'd been up a season or two. But we felt it was too much of a risk. They never made a concrete financial offer, either. It was all, "What do you want? What do you want?" when we were at the stage where we wanted to listen to offers.

'Gary wasn't completely set on coming back to England, and I think it's fair to say that if we had had Juventus, Inter Milan or Milan in, he would have gone to one of them. But they hadn't come in. In the meantime, in fact, Inter had got the Germans [Matthäus, Brehme and Klinsmann], Milan had got the Dutchmen [Gullit, Rijkaard and Van Basten] and Juventus had had a bad experience with Ian Rush and probably gone anti-British at that point. We kept hearing that Agnelli [Gianni Agnelli, head of the Fiat empire and owner of Juventus] wanted Gary. We were told he was going to contact us, but no-one ever came. So, we contacted Terry Venables [then manager of Tottenham Hotspur]. I rang him up, said Gary might fancy coming back to England and suggested a meeting.

Terry asked what Gary would want and I outlined a deal. He said he would put it to Irving Scholar [then the Tottenham chairman] and see what happened. He did and they came back. They fiddled about with it a little bit, but they didn't really contest it. I was telling them the fee was quite low, and they said, "OK, if you can get him for that sort of money, we'll have him." I said, "That's the advantage you've got: you are not going to have to pay that much."

'The fee was £1.1 million, and he was a steal at that. Barcelona were cheated in a sense, but I think they acknowledged to a degree that they were in a bit of a cleft stick. Cruyff wanted him out, and if we couldn't do a deal with anyone but Spurs, they were stuck with Spurs. So, we did the deal. At one point, Spurs looked like they were going to fall out of bed, and we did contact Manchester United; but they weren't interested. I told them what the financial package was and again they said they couldn't manage that at the time. So United missed out on Gary twice, really. There weren't any other serious candidates, although everyone thought Arsenal would go for him. We thought Arsenal would be the perfect fit, but we heard through a third party that George Graham [the Arsenal manager] wasn't interested because of the effect it might have on his wage structure. Anyway, Gary had come to the conclusion that he'd quite like to go to Spurs. One reason was that he'd got to go to a coach who understood what he was doing.'

Back in Barcelona, Graham Turner was still reeling from all the transfer comings and goings. 'There was one comic day,' he recalls, 'when Fiorentina, Monaco and Tottenham all had their representatives in the same hotel, the Princesa Sofia. I was actually sitting in the bar having a beer with the three agents. It was one meeting after another. Scooting off to one room and coming back; then going upstairs for another meeting.'

There is no doubt that Lineker left an indelible impression on the city of Barcelona and on Spain in general. Even now, Turner reveals, Spaniards are keen to join the Gary Lineker Fan Club. 'Michelle and I used to split the work of answering Gary's fan mail,' he says. 'I know it sounds a bit silly, but there were times when you were stashed away in a hotel, bored to tears, and you thought you might just as well be doing something. That was the time when Gary signed his first boot deal with Quaser. I've still got some of the autograph cards they produced, and I still get letters asking to join the Gary Lineker Fan Club. When they started it in England, I wondered whether anyone in Spain would be interested and did it as a little story for the two sports dailies in Barcelona. Suddenly, all this post started coming in, and it cost me a fortune in envelopes to answer the letters – sending cheques to England, cashing postal orders and so on. I've still got a shoe-box marked GLFC with all the counterfoils for payments. They must run into three figures.'

There were repercussions for Johan Cruyff, too, none of them very pleasant. They included a swingeing attack on him by Javier Clemente, now the manager of Spain who, in September 1992, began with his country's first victory over England on Spanish soil for 32 years. Back in June 1989, however, Clemente was coach of Atletico Madrid and commenting on Barcelona's purchase of Michael Laudrup (to replace Lineker) and a Brazilian defender called Aloisio. 'If Johan Cruyff thinks Aloisio is worth £1.5 million and sells Gary Lineker for less, then he is suggesting to me he knows very little about football,' said the outspoken Clemente. 'I would never think of selling Lineker, and I would never deliberately try to make a player fail. Lineker can never be a winger.'

The decision to sell Lineker certainly provoked something of a crisis on the Barcelona board and, in September 1989, it was rumoured in the Spanish media that Cruyff was about to be sacked and replaced by Luis Aragones, the manager who had succeeded Venables and preceded Cruyff. The idiosyncratic Dutchman survived, of course, and took the club on to greater glory. His 1992 triumph of bringing the European Cup to Barcelona for the first time not only enhanced his reputation as one of the most successful managers in football history, but made him virtually unsackable at the Nou Camp. Even then, though, he was not prepared to talk at length about the Lineker episode. 'There's nothing much to say,' Cruyff replied towards the end of 1992. 'He was a very nice person and we never had any problems; but he just didn't fit into my system.'

· 7 ·

Tottenham – Devalued
Dreams

When Gary Lineker, relieved to have escaped at last from the dis-
approving gaze of Johan Cruyff, agreed in the summer of 1989 to
return to England, he was fully entitled to believe his new club,
Tottenham Hotspur, were poised to make a major assault on
English football's most glittering prizes. After two seasons spent
getting the playing staff to his liking, it seemed Terry Venables
could now field a team that included not only Lineker, but Chris
Waddle, inherited from a previous manager, Peter Shreeves, and
Paul Gascoigne, signed from Newcastle United for £2 million the
previous year. It was certainly a mouth-watering prospect for the
fans of the London club: England's deadliest marksman fed with
ammunition by two of England's most creative midfielders.

Unfortunately, it did not work out quite like that. Before this
golden triangle could be put to work at White Hart Lane, Waddle
was sold to Marseille for £4.25 million. The reason was quite
simple: Spurs needed the money. Not many people knew it at the
time, but the brave new financial world football club chairman
Irving Scholar and his cohorts had established at Tottenham had
begun to run into serious financial difficulties. The football side of
the business was still in profit, but the parent company established
to exploit the commercial potential of the famous north London
club was starting to lose money on a massive scale.

It emerged later that Scholar had been worried about the overall
health of the company for a year before the hurried sale of Waddle.
That transfer was the first public alarm bell, but it was not until
more than a year afterwards, in September 1990, that the enormity
of Tottenham's plight became evident to all. Quite suddenly it
emerged that the first British club to become a public company,
the club supposedly showing the way ahead to all the others, was

anything between £13 and £23 million in debt, depending on which newspaper you read.

So bad did the situation become that, on Friday 19 October, 1990, the Stock Exchange suspended dealings in the shares of the parent company, Tottenham Hotspur plc, because factors that were likely to affect the share price had been concealed. As Alex Fynn and Lynton Guest put it in *Heroes and Villians*, their fascinating, fly-on-the-wall account of the 1990–91 season at Arsenal and Tottenham: 'The club that had made history in 1983 by becoming the first British football club to go public, a move seen by many at the time as a model for the future, had reached the point of collapse, its financial affairs in disarray, its board of directors in open confrontation with each other. The significance of the intervention by the Stock Exchange was that it underlined the fact that the directors had not only failed to establish a sound financial basis for the club but had compounded that failure by excessive secrecy.'

There followed a long, drawn-out battle for survival, and for control of the club. In the end, it came down to a straight fight between the late Robert Maxwell, the domineering, larger-than-life newspaper and publishing tycoon, and the financial partnership Venables formed for the purpose with Alan Sugar, millionaire boss of Amstrad Electronics. After some pretty fierce wheeling and dealing, Venables and Sugar called a press conference on Saturday 23 June, 1991, to announce they had reached agreement with the board of Tottenham Hotspur and the Stock Exchange to purchase the shares of Irving Scholar and Paul Bobroff, chairman of the plc, for £3.75 million. In view of the murky revelations about Maxwell's business conduct that followed his apparent suicide on 5 November, 1991 – and his cavalier treatment of Derby County, one of the clubs he had owned previously – there is no doubt that Spurs were fortunate in having Venables and Sugar fight it out with him to the bitter end.

Thus Venables, a former Spurs player, became the first English football manager to own his own club and Scholar, the wealthy property developer who had launched a takeover bid in 1981 because he was convinced Tottenham were headed for bankruptcy under the previous board unless someone like himself intervened, had to leave. It was sad in a way because, whatever his shortcomings in this matter, Scholar was a true Spurs fan who had only the club's best interests at heart. In his enthusiasm to make Tottenham successful, however, he overstepped the mark in more than one direction, not least that of allegedly interfering in team affairs.

This, then, was the troubled, unstable, unsettling background against which Gary Lineker played out the last three seasons of his career with the London club. The politics at White Hart Lane become almost as Byzantine as those at the Nou Camp and, at one point, Tottenham even had difficulty paying Barcelona the final instalment on the relatively modest joint transfer fee of £1.5 million they had agreed for Lineker and Mohamed Ali Amar, better known as Nayim. There were constant rumours, too, that both Lineker and Gascoigne would have to be sold to balance the books. In the end, of course, that is exactly what did happen.

It was all the more remarkable, therefore, that Lineker, between the advanced ages for a footballer of 28 and 31, should continue to score goals at a phenomenal rate and that Tottenham should finish third in the old First Division in 1989–90 and win the FA Cup in 1991. For despite the undoubted gifts of Lineker and Gascoigne, and the purchase of players such as Paul Stewart and Erik Thorst-vedt, this proved to be a fairly ordinary Spurs team by the high standards of some of their illustrious predecessors, especially when Gascoigne was missing for the whole of that final season, 1991–92, because of his serious knee injury.

There is no question that Lineker felt betrayed from the start. Re-calling a conversation with Venables during the 1990–91 season, Jon Holmes says: 'I told him Spurs hadn't developed in the way Gary had wanted when he came to the club. He'd been misled really by Irving Scholar, because we didn't know about the Waddle deal. Whether Irving knew or not, I don't know. Terry still thinks he didn't know about it before they signed Gary. But he did promise us that all the money would be re-spent on the team. And, of course, it wasn't. Gary had wanted to win medals with Spurs, but it didn't work out.' Lineker himself had stressed the importance he attached to playing with Waddle when he said: 'He knows my game, sees my runs and provides the most accurate passes I've ever had.'

Venables takes up the story of the Waddle business by saying: 'We'd turned down a lot of money for him – it had got to £4.25 million. And it was after we'd signed Gary. There were rumours that it was going on before, but that was definitely not true. I never knew about it, nor did Irving Scholar. But then they told me I had the lion's share of the £4.25 million to strengthen the team. I felt we could be fifth or sixth in the table with the money for Chris Waddle, which I was led to believe we could put into defenders. It could even have meant us challenging for the League title.

'But the money didn't materialise, and I felt hard done by. Whether they knew at the time they couldn't spare the money for players, or whether it was bad luck with the bank, I don't know. But that actually slaughtered me because I didn't have Chris Waddle and I didn't have the money. As the saying goes "I want the player or the money: I don't want the bit in the middle." But that's what we ended up with – the bit in the middle. I think the club – Irving – wanted some of the money for the bank and some of the money for players, but it didn't happen that way: that was the problem.'

Even if Venables had received the money he'd been promised, he might have struggled to spend it on the defenders he clearly believed Tottenham needed. For Irving Scholar was a jealous guardian of the club's reputation for open, imaginative, entertaining football. 'Irving was always happy to spend money on goalscorers,' says Venables, 'but he was not so keen on defenders. But if you score three goals and let in four, we all know what that means. He just wanted the entertainer, the box-office draw, which is OK. But there's got to be some hard common-sense in there as well.'

Venables's allegations on this subject are supported by stories of Scholar's refusal to back his manager's moves for Terry Butcher, then with Glasgow Rangers, and Mark Wright, then of Derby, on the grounds of cost. According to Messrs Fynn and Guest in *Heroes and Villains*, Venables was so desperate to sign a high-class defender that he even 'toyed with the idea of offering Gary Lineker to Derby in exchange for Wright and Dean Saunders, but the deal never got off the ground as there was no chance of Spurs raising the cash adjustment that would be required.'

The board did allow Venables to spend £1.4 million – a trifling amount for a club with serious title aspirations – on two defenders, Steve Sedgley and Pat van den Hauwe, in the summer of 1989, and their arrival helped stem the leaking of goals which had undermined the side since Richard Gough's return to Scotland in 1988. Indeed, Scholar must have felt his policy of financial restraint perfectly justified when Tottenham finished the 1989–90 season in third place behind Liverpool and Aston Villa and, perhaps more importantly, in front of Arsenal and Chelsea.

But a lot of that success was due to Lineker's amazing accuracy in front of goal. Readjusting immediately to English football, the ex-Leicester and Everton striker scored 24 times in his 38 League matches. It was a huge proportion of Tottenham's 59 League goals that season and dwarfed the contribution of the next highest scorer, Paul Stewart, who got only eight. Lineker was at his most consistent during Spurs final sprint for the finishing line. He scored six goals as Tottenham won all but one of their last eight games and climbed from ninth place to third.

Hopes were undoubtedly high at the start of the 1990–91 season. Despite sharing the fans' disappointment at the club's failure to come up with any money to strengthen the side in the close season, Venables was quoted as saying: 'I feel we have an improvement without a doubt. I think we've got a side now that's full of optimism, not only from the club but from the supporters. We've got excitement now. People want to watch us home and away.'

Such optimism and self-regard seemed thoroughly justified when Spurs began the season by going 10 games without defeat, scoring 17 goals and conceding only four. The device of playing David Howells in front of the back four increased the team's options in both defence and attack. In particular, it allowed Gascoigne, a national hero after his tearful heroics for England at the 1990 World Cup finals in Italy, greater freedom to go forward. The often electrifying Gazza responded with 19 League and cup goals, a total matched only by a Lineker less voracious and accurate than usual.

Despite that promising start, Tottenham's League form dipped after Christmas, and they slid down gradually from third place to tenth. Maybe that was partly because of two long cup runs. This was a season ending in a one (i.e. 1990–91), of course, and history has decreed that, more often than not, Tottenham should win the FA Cup at such a time.

Thanks largely to Gascoigne's inspired play, they made good progress in both the League (Rumbelows) Cup and the FA Cup. Gazza scored all but one of his side's goals as Spurs got off to a flying start in the Rumbelows Cup with a 5–0 trouncing of Hartlepool, then in the old Fourth Division. The Geordie imp scored again in each of the next two rounds, too, helping to see off Bradford City and Sheffield United before the run came to a crashing and unexpected halt with a 3–0 home defeat by Chelsea in a fifth-round replay.

That was shortly after a Paul Stewart goal had launched Tottenham's FA Cup campaign with a 1–0 third-round win at Blackpool. Then Gascoigne got back into scoring mode, claiming two goals each time as Oxford were defeated 4–2 and Portsmouth 2–1. Notts County were Spurs' quarter-final opponents, and Gascoigne scored one of the goals that gave the London club a 2–1 victory over their then Second Division opponents.

It was just before the sixth-round tie against Notts County that the news broke of Lazio's original £8 million bid for Gascoigne. Venables was furious, both at the timing of the story and because he knew nothing of the bid. The negotiations, clearly, had been carried out behind the manager's back, and only strengthened his determination to succeed with the plans he was beginning to lay for buying control of the club.

Another problem for Venables at the time was the hernia operation Gascoigne was obliged to undergo immediately after the sixth round to repair an injury he had been carrying for some time. Would he be fit for the FA Cup semi-final? All of Britain, never mind north London, wanted to know because the draw had pitted Tottenham against Arsenal in a tie of such magnitude that the Football Association decided to break with tradition and stage the game at Wembley Stadium to accommodate in comfort and safety all who wanted to see it. Somehow, Gascoigne recovered quickly enough to play. Only 31 days after the operation, and four days before the date with Arsenal, he proved himself ready for the semi-final by playing for an hour in Tottenham's 2–1 League defeat at Norwich.

And so the scene was set for one of the most thrilling and memorable contests in the recent history of English football. What gave it added piquancy was that Arsenal were leading the First Division and chasing the double. Tottenham, on the other hand, could be said to be playing for their lives, or at least their existence as a club. So deeply in debt were they, they needed to raise every penny they could from the FA Cup to keep the bailiffs from the door.

With Arsenal beaten only once all season in the League and Tottenham fielding two players, Gascoigne and Howells, only recently returned from long spells out, the bookmakers had no trouble choosing a favourite. Yet, after only five minutes, Gascoigne transformed the situation with the sheer brilliance of his talent. Taking a free-kick 35 yards out, the Tottenham midfielder struck the ball with such power, accuracy and curvature that David Seaman, the Arsenal goalkeeper, could not stop the shot even though he got a hand to it. Just before the kick, Lineker ran up to his hyperactive team-mate and told him that if he was going to have a dig not to try anything fancy, just hit the ball hard. But Gazza being Gazza, he could not resist scoring without a bit of a flourish.

Venables raved about the quality of the goal. 'All things put together, it added up to one of the best free-kicks ever seen (at Wembley) in all its history. It's easy to bend a ball and lack pace, or

74

just to curl it. But to bend it with power and accuracy is very special, especially from that distance. Schuster (his German midfielder at Barcelona) was fantastic. He could slog them as well with the bend. The two of them (Gascoigne and Schuster) are the best I've seen.'

Not satisfied with that *tour de force*, Gascoigne then set Paul Allen free on the right with some twinkling footwork. Allen's low centre caused enough chaos in the Arsenal goalmouth for Lineker to pounce and put Spurs 2–0 up. They were looking the hungrier and sharper team, yet Arsenal still managed to pull a goal back before the interval, Alan Smith heading a Lee Dixon centre past Thorstvedt. In the second half, the Gunners went looking for an equaliser with an intensity that left them vulnerable to a quick counter-attack by Tottenham.

Sure enough, with 14 minutes remaining, Lineker ran at Arsenal from the half way line while Vinny Samways made a decoy run to draw defenders away from the striker. Evading Tony Adams's attempted tackle, Lineker broke into the penalty area and delivered a shot that Seaman really ought to have saved. Again the Arsenal goalkeeper made contact, this time with both hands, but the ball hit the inside of a post and bounced into the net. Arsenal's quest for the double was over.

The euphoria did not last long. It was soon dispersed by the re-emergence of Spurs's twin problems – the proposed sale of the club and of Paul Gascoigne, to which Venables had declared himself utterly opposed. The future of the club remained unresolved before the FA Cup final on 18 May, when Tottenham were to meet Brian Clough's Nottingham Forest at Wembley, but Spurs officially signed away their interest in Gascoigne to Lazio. There was still some doubt about the transfer, since the player had yet to sign his personal contract, but arrangements were made for the Rome club to parade their new English capture at the club's final home game of the season, against Sampdoria on 26 May. It was, of course, the worst possible way to prepare for an FA Cup final.

Less than 24 hours before the most important match of Tottenham's season, a number of key people at the club were still trying to negotiate its sale. There was another pre-match upset, too, when the *Sun* reported that Spurs had been hawking Lineker around a number of Italian clubs. The story, though three months old, was true in that Dennis Roach, the international football agent, had been authorised to investigate the interest Napoli had been showing in the England captain. The only trouble was, neither Lineker nor Venables knew anything about it and the player, naturally enough, was extremely upset when he heard about this apparent attempt to sell him behind his back.

But that was as nothing to what happened in the final itself. Gascoigne, on whom the pressures of the transfer to Lazio and of winning the cup for Spurs had been building and building, finally flipped his lid. Hardly had the game started than this extremely volatile character had planted his studs in Garry Parker's chest with a full swing of the leg. Allowed to go unpunished by referee Roger Milford for that dangerous foul, Gascoigne then chopped down Gary Charles as the Nottingham Forest right-back made a run inside across the edge of the Tottenham penalty area. It was a double disaster for Spurs in that Stuart Pearce lashed home the free-kick and Gascoigne collapsed at the restart, his right knee wrecked by that wild tackle on Charles.

It looked all over for the London club in more ways than one. Gascoigne's departure on a stretcher after only 15 minutes robbed them of not only their likely match-winner, but possibly their immediate financial salvation as well, bearing in mind the size of the fee Lazio had agreed to pay for him. Yet Tottenham, as they had been doing throughout that remarkable, embattled season, again beat the odds. 'The players had to make a decision when Gazza went off,' Venables said later. 'Either that's us gone and people will understand if we lose, or, roll up our sleeves and do it for ourselves and for him.' Needless to say, they rolled up their sleeves.

Driven on and inspired by Paul Stewart, picking up the baton of midfield leadership from Gascoigne, Spurs twice went close to equalising before the interval, each time through Lineker. First he tucked away an Allen centre, only to find himself ruled offside – a decision proved incorrect by television's action replays. Then, brought down by Mark Crossley while rounding the Forest goalkeeper, Lineker was denied a goal from the penalty spot by Crossley's superb diving save. And still these 'southern softies' refused to give in.

Seven minutes into the second half, a quick, incisive move between Nayim, Gascoigne's replacement, and Allen opened up the Forest goal for Stewart to bury a low cross-shot behind Crossley. From then onwards, Tottenham were in control. Lineker was only one of many heroes as they ran their hearts out in search of a winning goal. It came finally in extra time. A corner kick by Nayim, flicked on by Stewart, saw the ultra-reliable Des Walker, of all people, head the ball into his own net in an attempt to stop Gary Mabbutt reaching it as the Spurs captain steamed in at the far post.

For Mabbutt, a nice man and a good player, it was the crowning moment of his long career with Spurs. 'This means everything to me,' he said, 'because I've been at Tottenham nine years and only ever got a UEFA Cup medal. In 1987, losing the FA Cup (to Coventry) really was difficult to take, but coming here to win today as captain has made up for that.' Lineker, who described the achievement at the time as his 'best moment in footall', later nominated Spurs's FA Cup semi-final and final victories as two of his three outstanding memories at club level (the other was winning the Cup-Winner's Cup with Barcelona). 'Since we played both games at Wembley,' he said, 'it was like winning the cup twice.'

Venables did not equivocate. 'I would say this is my finest achievement as a manager, especially given the year we've had,' he said with a certainty that did not apply to his or the club's future. Everything was up in the air now. Fortunately for Tottenham, Lazio maintained their interest in Gascoigne and agreed to pay a reduced fee of £5.5 million for him provided he recovered fully from his terrible injury. A proportion of the money paid in advance helped placate the Midland Bank, Spurs's principal creditor, but Venables scoffed at word that a new one-year contract worth £300,000 was to be offered him by Scholar and talked of leaving unless he could win total control of the club.

Against all expectation, he succeeded in doing precisely that little more than a month after Tottenham's stirring triumph over Nottingham Forest at Wembley. Although technically outbid by Maxwell, the Venables-Sugar partnership was preferred by the Tottenham board largely because they feared mass disaffection among the fans if Venables left and Scholar, who was seen as being responsible for the club's financial plight in the first place, was joined by Maxwell, a fickle, unpredictable 'benefactor' few football supporters trusted.

But the management buy-out was only the first step towards pulling the great old club round. Without Gascoigne (whose injury, and a further scrape in a Newcastle nightclub, put him out of football for the next 17 months), and without most of the money for Gascoigne, Venables was again left with the 'bit in the middle'. Nevertheless, he did manage to scrape together the £2 million needed to buy Gordon Durie, the powerful Scottish international striker, from Chelsea and provide Lineker with a new partner for the 1991–92 season.

They hit it off immediately. In the first seven League games, five of them won, Lineker scored 11 goals and Durie two. In the last of those matches, a remarkable 5–3 victory away to Wimbledon, the England captain claimed four. He amassed another 17 over the rest of the season, finishing with the truly awesome figures of 28 goals in 35 League appearances. Only a hat-trick – two of the goals coming in the last minute – on the last day of the season by Arsenal's Ian Wright, who scored 29 League goals in all for Crystal Palace and Arsenal, stopped Lineker ending his career as the leading scorer in the Football League for the fourth time.

He will have been disappointed not to have gone out at the top of the list, since he has always measured his success at club level in terms of League goals. Talking about the three occasions on which he had been the League's leading scorer (1984–85 with Leicester (24), 1985–86 with Everton (30) and 1989–90 with Tottenham (24)), he said: 'As a striker, you've got to want to be the best, and I've always had a lot of ambition. At the start of every season, I've always wanted to be the top goalscorer. League goals are the most important thing because some players don't play too many cup games. It's the fairest yardstick, too, because you are always playing against the top clubs. It's only through playing on the Continent I've got into that way of thinking, because they don't even talk about cup goals over there. But they make quite a big thing about being top scorer in the League.'

Thus, it is almost as an afterthought one mentions that Lineker also contributed five of the 14 goals Tottenham scored in their run to the semi-finals of the Rumbelows Cup (now the Coca-Cola Cup), and two of the five they scored before being knocked out of the European Cup-Winner's Cup in the quarter-finals by Feyenoord – making a grand total of 35 for the season. Little wonder, then, that the football writers of England voted, at season's end, to give him their coveted 'Footballer of the Year' award as a going-away present. It made him only the sixth player in the 44-year history of the award to win it twice. The previous time had been in 1985–86, when he was scoring all those goals with Everton and swept the board by being elected Player of the Year by his fellow professionals as well.

Ironically, in view of what had happened the previous May, Nottingham Forest were the team who stopped a Gazza-less Spurs returning to Wembley in the Rumbelows Cup. After being held to a 1–1 draw in the first leg at the City Ground, Forest won that semi-

final with a stirring 2–1 victory in atrociously wet and muddy conditions at White Hart Lane, Lineker's goal for Tottenham not being
enough. That exhausting contest could well have cost Spurs their
place in the Cup-Winner's Cup, too, because the overcrowded
English fixture list forced them to play it only three days before
going to Rotterdam, where they lost the first leg of their Cup-
Winners' Cup tie 1–0 to Feyenoord.

The regularity of Lineker's scoring that season was made all the
more astonishing by two other major considerations. One of them
was the generally undistinguished form of the team in which he was
playing. Without the ebullience and inventiveness of Gascoigne,
Spurs gradually slid from third place in the table in late September
to fifteenth by the following May. That final position represented
something of a recovery, because they had sunk dangerously close
to the relegation zone in March and April.

Since Lineker scored ten of his goals in the club's last ten difficult
League matches, his team-mates were well aware of the contribution he had made to the rescue act. 'With Gary in the side,' says
Gary Mabbutt, Spurs' captain, 'you always knew that, even if the
team wasn't playing particularly well and things weren't going well
for us, we were liable to get a result because, in a 90-minute game,
there was a very good chance he would score for you. It gives you
an air of confidence. Like last season (1991–92): the team wasn't
playing particularly well, but Gary was still very nearly the highest
scorer in the League.

'In fact, he's never let anyone down when the pressure's been on.
Look at when he took those penalties against Cameroon in the
1990 World Cup finals, or the goal he scored in Poland when
England qualified for Sweden. It must be the mark of a world-class
player when you look at the records and see that from the very
beginning, in his case the days at Leicester, to playing for England in
the World Cup finals, he has scored goals. He's done it at every possible level, and that speaks volumes for his ability.'

Courage and strength of character also came into the equation
that season where Lineker was concerned. For in late November
1991, it was discovered that his son, George, born little more than a
month earlier, was suffering from acute myeloid leukaemia, a rare
form of the disease. It was a brutal blow that sent the well-ordered
world of the Linekers, and that of their family and close friends,
spinning into a vortex of grief, anxiety and confusion for what must
have seemed an age.

Gary told the story of that dreadful episode most vividly in an interview with Hunter Davies, the novelist, journalist and keen football fan, in the *Independent* in May 1992. Davies pointed out that, with Gary aged 31 and Michelle 27, it was quite late for them to have a first baby, but explained they had decided to wait a while before starting a family, preferably until they were back in England. That is how George came to be born in London on 2 October, 1991. He weighed 8lb 9oz and looked perfectly healthy until just before England's crucial European Championship qualifying match in Poland on 13 November.

'Michelle rang me in Poland,' Lineker told Davies, 'and said she could feel a little lump on his head. She thought perhaps it was nothing, just a spot which would go. When I got home, there seemed to be more lumps, so we took him to the doctor. They thought it was a skin infection at first and gave him antibiotics, but that didn't clear it up. They did a biopsy, still 90 per cent sure it was just a skin infection, then a few days later he started looking very pale and his glands began swelling. That's when they knew it was leukaemia. Acute myeloid leukaemia. I know all the different sorts now. You become a sort of expert when all this happens. The chances of his survival at the time were under 50 per cent.

'Since then, he's been having chemotherapy treatment. That upsets the body's antibodies, but luckily Michelle has been able to keep feeding him herself. We hope this is the last course of chemo-therapy. Technically, he's in remission at the moment. The hospital [the world-famous Great Ormond Street Hospital for Sick Children] has been very good, very straight, told us everything.

'The first few weeks were a nightmare. I couldn't sleep, couldn't think of anything else. I went through all sorts of emotions. The biggest was fear. Sometimes I was down, and Michelle would help me. Then it was the other way round. We did despair when it seemed touch and go. You just have to be positive, believe he will be OK, remain optimistic.'

Davies asked Lineker whether the experience had made him turn to religion, or perhaps encouraged him to take the cynical view that what had happened to George was some kind of judgment on him, Gary Lineker, for having had more than his fair share of good fortune up to then. Lineker replied that he had prayed a lot, but that Michelle had leaned more heavily on religion than he had. As for the second part of the question, he said: 'That thought did strike me, but I know it's not true. I only have to look around to realise that. These things happen to good and bad people, rich and poor, black and white, lucky and unlucky. It's random chance, for no good reason. I know I've had a lucky life, but that's not connected with what's happened.'

Jon Holmes certainly admits to dark thoughts about the episode. 'You feel it's some sort of revenge, don't you?' he says. ' "You've done all right, so this is your bill", kind of thing. The way it happened, it knocked everyone sideways. They have coped with it really well, but it needed a major effort from Gary to deal with it. They recovered quite quickly, but for a day he couldn't say anything: he just couldn't speak. Gradually, he came round from that. It was a very shattering thing for me in a way, being so close to him over a period of time. He had to be talked through it to a degree. Michelle was unbelievably tough, and together they managed. It was a difficult period for them, and it might still be difficult. We are not out of the woods yet, although you'd like to think they've overcome the worst.'

The one thing everyone agrees on is the immense courage, devotion and steadfastness shown throughout by Michelle Lineker. 'That was a very traumatic time in their lives,' says Barry Lineker, Gary's father. 'I don't know how they coped – well, I don't know how Michelle coped with it, really. She was unbelievable. She just lived at the hospital for about six months.' Michelle would spend most of every day and all of every night at Great Ormond Street. She slept on a camp bed. Gary would join her every day, sit with George, have a meal, see George asleep, kiss his wife goodnight and then go home alone to an empty house.

It goes without saying that Lineker was not in any fit state mentally or emotionally to play any football for a while. Tottenham, supportive throughout, gave him leave of absence for as long as he wanted. Terry Venables, an emotional man under that streetwise Cockney exterior, felt the pain of the experience as keenly as anyone. 'When I went round there to see him when it first happened,' he recalls, 'I just felt so helpless. You couldn't really comfort him. He just didn't know what had hit him. I just felt so sorry for both of them. No-one deserves that. It was such a shame. It's difficult to explain, because something like that is so horrific you can't put any sense to it. It just goes to show that the worst thing can happen to people who actually seem to have everything.'

Lineker's powers of recovery were such that he missed only three League matches and one Rumbelows Cup tie. It was as if he needed to start playing again to take his mind off his personal problems. At all events, he returned in Tottenham's live televised game against Liverpool at White Hart Lane on 18 December, just over three weeks after his last previous appearance. It was not where he would have chosen to restart his season, but fog had stopped him flying up to Leeds a few days earlier to play for Spurs at Elland Road.

'Liverpool was not the ideal match,' he agreed afterwards. 'Basically, I wanted to go out on the pitch and play without creating a stir. Unfortunately the fog meant the 'plane to Leeds was cancelled, and I never made it. The game against Liverpool was slightly more high profile, and I found it as hard a game as I have played, both mentally and physically. When you sit in a hospital for two weeks without doing anything, you need a couple of matches to get fit.'

It was hardly the moment to be measuring your popularity, but the thousands and thousands of letters the Linekers received from well-wishers must have left them in no doubt of the high regard in which Gary is held by a large proportion of the population. 'Football's important to me,' Lineker said in a *Sunday Times* interview with Rob Hughes at the time, 'but you would have to be an oddball not to realise there are wars and people dying of famine. It has taken this horrible disease happening to George to show us that the vast majority of people are caring, kind people. It would be impossible for us to answer all the letters that we've had, but many of them reaffirm your faith in human nature. I have always realised that football is not the most important thing in the world.'

Lineker was also deeply appreciative of the reaction of the Tottenham fans. 'They have been great, particularly since the personal problem I've had,' he said near the end of the 1991–92 season. 'They've been very supportive and I've had thousands of letters from them. Even though I didn't play for a while, I got great ovations when I came back. They've been very encouraging even though in the early games it was difficult for me, perhaps I wasn't firing on all cylinders. They were patient and understanding, and I appreciate that. I think it gives you a bit more of a special feeling than you would have towards the club normally.'

By the time Lineker's son fell ill, of course, Venables was no longer manager of Spurs. Having won control of the club, he became its chief executive and gave Peter Shreeves, manager from 1984 to 1986, his second spell in charge. So it was left to Shreeves to say after the Liverpool match: 'Gary was his alert self before the game and, although physically tired at the end, I am sure he was delighted to have got that game out of the way.' Graeme Souness, the Liverpool manager, was also sympathetic. 'It must have been an enormous decision for Gary,' he said, 'and everyone's thoughts in football are with him. I know that is true of my club.'

Shreeves, who is coach to the Welsh national team and has seen the Wales manager, Terry Yorath, fight his way through the terrible experience of having his teenage son die suddenly and unexpectedly in his arms because of a rare heart defect, is equally full of compassion and admiration for Lineker. 'To do what Gary did in that one season, and score the goals he did for his club and his country and still get on with his personal problems, shows the character of the boy, really,' he says. 'He wasn't one of those lads you could put a downer on.'

Shreeves was sacked by Spurs at the end of the 1991–92 season, and the rumours coming out of White Hart Lane suggested that he felt Lineker could have worked harder for the team. But the former Tottenham manager, a decent, honourable man who finds it difficult to say anything nasty about anyone, refuses to substantiate those stories. Venables speaks for him on the subject when he says: 'I've been through what Peter's been through, and you can agree that Gary's going through a barren spell and not working like the others; but that was his style, like Peter Osgood and Martin Chivers. When they were playing well, they weren't knocking people over, and Gary's style is exactly the same. Jimmy Greaves was even worse, if you are going to talk about that side of it.'

Shreeves himself takes up the theme by saying, true to form: 'If you are going to win a championship in modern English football, you need twin strikers who are going to get you 40 goals between them; and Gary would always chip in with more than his share. Steve Archibald was another excellent player who didn't want to do the hurrying and the scurrying, but who more or less said: "Get the ball in the box, and I'll do the damage." And like Gary, he proved his point.' Just to underline his own view, Shreeves adds: 'Gary finished a difficult season for me getting 30-odd goals and more than contributing to his part of the play.'

If anyone still doubts that Shreeves has anything but the highest regard for Gary Lineker, they should think back a few years to his previous spell as manager. An examination of the records will show that Shreeves actually tried to buy Lineker at the time he was moving on from Leicester. 'I was about £5,000 off of getting him and making what I thought then was a team that would have won us the championship,' says Shreeves, no doubt running the names of Glenn Hoddle, Ossie Ardiles, Chris Waddle and other Spurs players of that time through his mind. 'He was then at Leicester, and we felt we needed just that extra one to make us into a unit.

'Gordon Milne was then the manager of Leicester, and I remember 'phoning him at Lilleshall. We couldn't agree over five grand, so it was a bit disappointing. It was one of those points of principle that often happens. Gary could have become a Spurs player before he did, but then he might not have gone on to do the Barcelona bit and all of that.'

Like Bobby Robson, Shreeves is in danger of getting carried away when he starts talking about Lineker's ability. 'Without any shadow of doubt,' he says, 'he was the best finisher I've seen at all the different clubs I've been at. I always felt he had a sort of inbuilt sixth sense, that he would forever know where he had to be while the build-up was occurring.

'After one game, I said something like: "In his mind he goes, yeah, if that ball goes there, then it's going to come here and that's where I'd better get myself." It may sound fairly basic, but that's how I saw it. Then, of course, he was technically good. He made all the right body shapes you teach youngsters on finishing. You know – head down, knee over the ball and things like that. So I'm sure someone in his younger days must have taught him that.

'He was as good on angled finishing as anybody I've seen. You know, you'd say: "He can't score from there," and he'd scream it in. Afterwards, the other team would say their goalie shouldn't have got beat on the near post; but he had, and he would again. Gary also scored goals all over the goal – high, low, little tickle here, little tickle there. But it was his anticipation that was his biggest gift.'

While at least one of Lineker's managers was irritated by his apparent distaste for training, Shreeves found nothing but fascination in the player's precise judgment of what physical preparation was needed to bring him to peak fitness on match days. 'The interesting thing, as I saw it with Gary, was that he knew exactly what his own body required. I was always amazed at how he managed to maintain his sharpness without doing any sharp work. He would only do that on a match day. He would have a long soak in the bath, then go out and do his warm-up.

'Other people I've worked with have stayed behind after training and done some sprinting on a daily basis. But he never did that in my time with him. Whether he did it elsewhere I don't know. It was a little bit surprising that he maintained such sharpness; but then again, with the rigours of our domestic season, he'd learned all about that.' Or, as Lineker himself put it on one occasion: 'There are too many games to train. How are you supposed to train when you should be improving your technique?'

Unprompted, Shreeves picks out another aspect of Lineker's play and personality that makes him different from the majority of strikers. 'He was not one that you would say of: "Well he might get one goal"; there were times you felt he might get a hat-trick for you. I don't think, in my coaching experience, I've come across that with anyone else. He was uncanny in that respect.'

And what of the final analysis? Where would Lineker figure in Shreeves's private strikers' Hall of Fame? 'In my time at Tottenham,' he says, 'we had Archie [Steve Archibald] and Garth Crooks. They were excellent, and I think Terry [Venables] thought Archie was as good as anyone he worked with. But I would have to put Links in front of them. I've worked with Ian Rush and Dean Saunders for Wales, and I would put him in front of Dean just at the minute. But it would be a fairly close-run race between Links and Rush.'

Venables, too, was prepared to make allowances for Lineker's unusual approach to training. Indeed, he once let him go away to Tenerife in the middle of a season for a spot of R & R. 'He is not keen on training,' says the Tottenham supremo, 'he believes he gets the best out of himself by holding back. I don't think I can dispute that, but I have to argue sometimes with the fact that the other players complain about it. But you've got to educate the others. If he's scoring goals – and that's the hardest thing in the game to do – you've got to say, "There's something in this!"'

'I took a chance when he was not doing very well, and gave him a week or ten days off on holiday while everyone else was training. There was a big risk factor involved, but he came back and, bosh, he was into the goals again. So it worked for me. But it was a big risk because you are running a big ship and these other people are looking, and I'm always very aware of that.'

Another member of the Spurs staff who backs Lineker's peculiar training regimen is John Sheridan, the highly regarded physiotherapist who played a major part in the rehabilitation of Paul Gascoigne following his catastrophic knee injury. Like a lot of other experts, Sheridan takes the view that Lineker knew exactly what his body needed to keep it in peak condition. 'He just used to take a lot of hot baths to get his muscles going [something a doctor at Leicester advised Lineker to do to improve poor circulation to his feet],' says Sheridan. 'He was a very, very fit fella. He knew what he had to do to keep going, and he proved it by going out on a Saturday and producing the goods time and again.

'When you are a senior pro at that level, and you've produced the goods consistently over the years, you should know exactly what sort of training you need to do. If he didn't train, he would often come into the treatment room and get on the bike, get his heart going and get a sweat on. So he would do work, but he knew what he was doing. In fact, I think he did more training than people give him credit for. He must have been doing something right.'

What has been common knowledge inside the game for some years, but not outside it, is that Lineker has had to overcome a nagging ache in the big toe of his right foot. It was a wear and tear injury that started in 1986, the year he was leading scorer in the Mexican World Cup finals, and became so bad at times that he tried every conceivable means of relieving the pain. Acupuncture was one remedy applied at Barcelona and continued by John Sheridan at Tottenham.

'It did help him quite a lot,' says the physio. 'It certainly helped to keep him going over the last season he was with Tottenham. We knew he needed acupuncture, and we knew there was no danger of causing a real problem by playing on it. It was just uncomfortable, but the acupuncture did relieve some of the symptoms. Acupuncture is very safe anyway, and we found that conventional therapies didn't really help the toe.'

Grampus Eight need not worry. Lineker had the problem resolved by an operation he underwent at London's Princess Grace Hospital in October 1992, to clean up the big toe joint, which was suffering from calcification and the intrusion of foreign bodies. Normally, for a footballer, it would take two or three months to recover fully from such an operation, and that is why Lineker did not have it done while he was in full-time employment in Spanish and English football. In other words, there never was the time, and the pain was bearable.

'Actually,' says John Sheridan, 'for a fellow that's played as long as Gary has, he's in superb condition. His joints are excellent, except for his big toe. He's taken a lot of stick from defenders, but he's hardly missed a game. It's very unusual for him to be injured. The only problem I ever had with him was his toe.'

Top left: *The way we were: long hair, acne, the lot. Gary Lineker poses for his picture early in that formative, seven-year period with Leicester City*

Top right: *Lineker, challenged by Gary Stevens and watched carefully by Steve Perryman, in First Division action for Leicester against Tottenham Hotspur*

Above: *Lineker wheels away in triumph after putting Everton ahead in the 1986 FA Cup final. Liverpool's Bruce Grobbelaar and Alan Hansen look on in dismay*

Left: *Spurs have cropped up frequently in Lineker's career. Here he scores against them the first of his 30 League goals for Everton in 1985–86*

Top: *The volley that completed the mos
important hat-trick of Lineker's career.
England beat Poland 3–0 to stay in the
1986 World Cup finals*
Left: *Lineker and Peter Beardsley celebr
England's 3–0 quarter-final victory over
Paraguay in the 1986 World Cup. The
attacking partners scored all three betwe
them*
Above: *One of the four goals by Lineke
that gave England a 4–2 victory over Sp
in 1987. 'Finishing of the highest calibre
Bobby Robson called it*

Above: *The good life, Spanish-style. Lineker and wife Michelle (far right) flank Mark Hughes as they relax on the beach with friends while at Barcelona*
Left: *Steve Archibald, the Scottish international striker Lineker was bought to replace at Barcelona, in European action for the Spanish club against Juventus*
Below: *Lineker, the reluctant winger, bursts between two opponents during Barcelona's 2–0 victory over Sampdoria in the final of the 1989 European Cup-Winners' Cup*

Above: *The intense pressures of managing Barcelona are illustrated vividly as Johan Cruyff, proud and impassive, gets the full treatment from press photographers*
Below: *Terry Venables and Irving Scholar (right) at the start of a manager-chairman relationship that deteriorated during the battle for control of hard-up Tottenham*
Opposite above: *Take that! Lineker stabs home the first of his two goals in Spurs' epic 3–1 win against Arsenal in the 1991 FA Cup semi-final at Wembley*
Opposite below left: *Paul Gascoigne rushes to hug Lineker at the end of the FA Cup semi-final against Arsenal in which they scored Tottenham's three goals between them*
Opposite below right: *Glory, glory, hallelujah! Lineker's pleasure shows as Spurs win the FA Cup by beating Nottingham Forest 2–1 and he collects his only major English medal*

Above: *Lineker scores England's equaliser against (West) Germany in the semi-finals of the 1990 World Cup, a game settled heartbreakingly by a penalty shoot-out*
Below left: *Training was not always a chore for Gary Lineker. He is obviously enjoying himself here with Peter Beardsley, Paul Gascoigne and a headless England team-mate*
Below right: *Lineker, wearing the captain's arm-band, in suitably sombre mood before England's fateful European Championship match against Sweden in Stockholm on 17 June, 1992*
Opposite above: *Lineker at his best, as he sends England to the finals of the 1992 European Championship with a spectacular volleyed equaliser against Poland in Poznan*

Opposite: *The bitter end. Gary Lin moments after being controversial. substituted in the match against Su*

Top: *Gary Lineker set to seize any half chance in the 1992 European Championship match against France which ended in a 0–0 draw*

Above: *Lineker, the master of public relations, poses with local children during his trip to Nagoya in August 1992 to play for Grampus Eight in a friendly*

Right: *A taste of things to come. Wearing the colours of his new Japanese club, Lineker makes one of the textbook body shapes Peter Shreeves admired so much*

Even so, the problem was troublesome enough to convince Jon Holmes that his client was doing the right thing by getting out of English football and going to Japan. 'We played golf at Sunningdale last summer [1991],' he recalled, 'and at the end of the round, Gary could hardly walk. I said to him: "Listen, I'm the unfittest man in the world. What's going on here?" And he said: "My toe's bloody killing me!" I thought: "Christ Almighty, if he can't walk round a golf course, there is something seriously wrong."'

For some time, it would appear, Lineker and his agent had been coming to the conclusion that he had had enough of English League football. 'We always thought,' says Holmes, 'the problem with someone who'd done what he's done was the way to go out. We talked about it a lot, and he said he wanted to go out at the top. "I don't want to go down the divisions, or anything like that," he stressed.

'The same thing applied to his international career. We always thought it was very sad about Bryan Robson, and the way things ended there. Peter Shilton did really well to go out right at the top. He didn't get dropped. He said: "Right, that's it," and declared. They seem to do it better abroad than we do here. Our managers seem to want their stars to play until they drop, so that they can prove who's boss.'

What crystallised the situation was the interest shown in Lineker by the fledgling Japanese professional clubs. For one thing, it made up Lineker's mind about his international career. 'We knew,' says Holmes, 'that when the Japanese came in, everybody would start asking questions about the international thing. So we thought, it's the European Championship, let's say that's it and cut out all the speculation and nonsense. Let's go for it.'

It was not quite that simple, of course. Clubs closer to home were keen to sign one of the world's leading goalscorers. 'Overtures were made from various parts of Europe,' admits Holmes, 'but in many ways Japan was a bigger challenge. It also gave Gary the opportunity to have a few months off. I was concerned about the number of games he was playing, and he was worried about his toe and all the other things that just grind the players to death.'

When Venables enquired about Lineker's willingness to go on beyond that third season at White Hart Lane, Holmes left him in no doubt that his client had had enough. 'When Terry asked me how he felt, I said: "Well, if it's a rebuilding job, I think he's going to find it hard to get motivated for that." Terry knew the score, and we told Spurs all the way about the Japanese interest. We said that if they weren't happy with the deal, Gary would be prepared to go on for the extra year with them. As far as international football was concerned, though, he didn't think he could do another World Cup. He felt that, for a striker of his age, it would be a tournament too far.'

The one thing Lineker was determined not to do was carry on playing in England to the bitter end while sliding down the scale all the time. 'Every player has to do what he thinks is right,' he said. 'It's not up to me to judge whether other players went on too long. Some players just like to keep playing at whatever level they possibly can, and that's fine by them. But I would find it exceptionally difficult to motivate myself at a lower level. I wanted to go out at the top and not somewhere below it. It's not always easy to judge when that is or will be, but it seems to be working out quite well. I believe it would be incredibly difficult to keep going until I was 33. I know my body.'

Sheer tiredness and waning motivation, rather than waning physical powers, were Lineker's main problems towards the end with Tottenham. Venables realised it, and it was almost certainly one of the reasons he decided not to block the player's plans to go to Japan for a big pay-day and the stimulus of a fresh challenge. 'The only problem with Gary at Tottenham,' says Venables, 'was that he found it really hard to motivate himself. He knew his own business so well, it didn't really hurt him. But you knew there was going to come a time when, because he'd had so many summers of no rest, he was going to get tired. These boys go off for two months, come back and I make them work very hard. Gary's had no rest. You can't do that – it's common-sense.

'In those three seasons at Tottenham, Gary was at the peak of his career. If he had the desire, he still would be now. Without that desire, it's irrelevant. I can understand his attitude. Life's not just about football, which is something he's always understood. At the end of a game when things had gone badly, he would make remarks like, "Well, it's only a game!" That's how he kept his head straight, and it works for him. But those around him get a little infuriated with that when it's perhaps more than a game for them. He's trying to say, "Well, let's get this in proportion: it's not the end of the world." But for lots of people, it is the end of the world at that moment. That sort of remark can upset you, especially when a manager's job is on the line.

'The difference is that he knows he's got enough in him to contribute outside the game and enjoy it just as much. He's intelligent enough to know he doesn't get the thrill he did before. I don't think he does. Not that other things ever got in the way of his football. It was just that he got tired. He's had too many games and too little rest. I think if Gary had got his proper rest for two months every year, like everyone else, he'd have played another two years here. I think it just caught up with him in the end. He was tired, mentally tired, and he'd had enough. That's why I don't think he's missed playing while he's been out of the game.'

While Venables is prepared to assess Lineker as objectively and candidly as that, and to hint at the friction the striker's laid-back attitude to life sometimes caused at Tottenham, he yields to no-one in his admiration for him as a person and as a player. 'I like him as a man,' says the only manager to have bought the striker twice. 'He knows what he's doing with his image, and why not? There's nothing wrong with that. I've had my disappointments with the way he played at certain times, and things that he did, but when you are signing off and saying he's not going to be here any more, you are going to give him a lot of marks out of 10. I don't think I can praise him more highly than that.'

Lineker and Jon Holmes are more than willing to return the compliment. Holmes treasures his relationship with Venables as an example of how manager and agent can work together sensibly and without rancour for the benefit of a player and his club, while Lineker is in no doubt that his former boss will bring back the glory, glory days to White Hart Lane. 'English clubs have to play so many games, often in heavy conditions, that you have got to have a big squad; and to be challenging for things like League titles, you've got to have a big squad full of good players.

'Due to the problems Tottenham have had financially over the years, they've not really been able to build on the players that were already there. So with players losing form – as everybody does in the course of a season – players getting injuries, suspensions and what have you, there hasn't really been the right quality to come in and the team suffered because of it. But I think – and I hope – that with Terry and Alan Sugar in charge, they are turning the corner and they'll be in a position where they can strengthen the side and broaden the squad. I'm sure they will progress. Terry knows what he's doing, and I'm sure they'll be successful again.'

Perhaps the last word on Lineker's three seasons with Tottenham should come from Peter Shreeves. Asked, towards the end of that final season for them both at White Hart Lane, how difficult it would be to replace the England striker, Shreeves replied succinctly and to the point – 'Mission impossible.'

· 8 ·

England – The Ecstasy

What Gary Lineker did for England, and what England did for Gary Lineker, was central to his whole career. While no-one would dispute that the striker made a profound impression at club level with Leicester, Everton, Barcelona and Tottenham, it was really his achievements with the national team that made him a household name. Once he had established himself in the national consciousness by scoring six goals in the finals of the 1986 World Cup – more than any of the world's best in Mexico that summer – he was there to stay.

When he continued to score with machine-like regularity, boyish enthusiasm and impeccable behaviour, his appeal transcended simple club loyalties: he became that soccer rarity, a true national hero. Here was 'Roy of the Rovers' made flesh for every feuding English football fan at a time when the forces of darkness – violence, greed and cynicism – appeared to be gaining the upper hand in world football. His timing could not have been better, on or off the field, and he was taken to the hearts of a populace hiding romantic ideals under a hard-bitten exterior.

The man who first made it all possible was Bobby Robson, that much-maligned former England manager of whom time has forced many to revise their opinions drastically. No doubt Lineker would have forced his way into the England side eventually, but the point is that Robson spotted the player's potential when he was still a bit raw with Leicester and brought him into the England squad as an investment for the future. This, remember, was a player without an international pedigree, a player who had not played for his country previously at youth or Under-21 levels.

While there were no great sums of money at stake in Robson's case, it is significant that the England manager was willing to back his judgment with his reputation at a time when several big, supposedly knowledgeable clubs were dithering over whether to buy this goalscoring young flier. If Bobby Robson, ex-manager of PSV Eindhoven and, at the time of writing, manager of the Portuguese club, Sporting Lisbon, has a fault, it is not his judgment of a player.

Lineker was called up by his country for the first time in late April, 1984. That was close to the end of Leicester's first season back in the First Division after two in the Second; a season that saw the striker score 22 goals in 39 League appearances. He was named in the squad for the game against Wales at Wrexham on 2 May in the expiring British Championship, but did not play in what turned out to be an embarrassing 1–0 defeat for England. Ironically, in view of their sharply differing fortunes at Barcelona a few years later, Wales's winning goal that day was scored by a certain Mark Hughes, then only 20 and making his international debut in his home town. But, not for the first or last time, circumstances worked in Lineker's favour.

'When I first saw Gary,' Robson recalls, 'he wasn't a great player: he'd just got in the Leicester side. But I noticed he had a certain quickness and sharpness about him. You know, just getting into front positions and getting behind defenders. He wasn't an accomplished player at the time: he just played in the last third [of the field]. He was a finisher-off of everything else that went on before. I spoke to Gerry Summers, the Leicester coach, about him. I'd played with Gerry at West Bromwich, and he, Don Howe [then England coach] and I were close friends. Gerry told me one or two things about Gary that pleased me. He said he was a prospect for the future, that he was going to be a goalscorer and maybe prolific. He was quick over five yards, he could read defenders, he could get behind defenders, he was very alive and quick to the ball in the box.

'I picked him for the first time in the squad – but didn't play him – when we played Wales in 1984. We had one or two injuries, and I brought him in just to have a look at him close up in training with Bryan Robson and the other big names who were in the England team at the time: Tony Woodcock and that type of guy. As it turned out, we lost 1–0 to the Welsh at Wrexham in one of our not very good performances. Hughes got the goal from a cross, and we played pretty dismally to be honest. Gary didn't play, as I've mentioned, but he still caught my eye as a member of the squad. It just went from there, really. He did better at Leicester, he improved and then got his move to Everton. From there, it was on to Barcelona and the big time.'

There is simply no disguising the depth of Robson's admiration for a player he had no hesitation in including in a 'Dream Team' of England players put together for the purposes of his 1990 autobiography, *Against The Odds*. 'He was just a natural goalscorer,' enthuses the former England manager. 'He didn't join in many movements but his first touch in the box was brilliant. Remarkably, his first touch inside the box was better than his first touch outside it. He just came alive when he was in the penalty area. He would join in, he'd hold the ball up, he'd keep it simple, he'd knock it back, spin and so forth, but he just loved it when people got in wide positions, got early crosses in and he could come across the centre-half and be first to the ball.

'He learned to play against the sweeper system as well. I think going to Barcelona helped, but he also met it in top international football. Not only was he good at coming in on stuff from wide positions, left or right, but he also learned how to get the wrong side – or right side, for him – of a marker. He had to because, as he got a bit of a name, a bit of a reputation, people were paying close attention to him. He learned how to get in front of a defender, show himself, then spin and get behind defenders.

'He was also quick to get on to the through ball. When he was in the team, we used to talk to Glenn Hoddle, Bryan Robson and Ray Wilkins – all the midfield players who played with him – about the importance of seeing his runs and hitting the ball into space between the two centre-halves. He wasn't a target-man, but you could knock it up to him and, as long as he kept it simple, realised what his assets were and didn't try to do anything complicated, he could be very efficient.'

Despite all these qualities, Lineker's early international career did not keep pace with his rapid progress at club level. Although Robson's dissatisfaction with the Wrexham performance saw the Leicester striker make his debut as a substitute for Woodcock in England's next match, a 1–1 draw with Scotland in Glasgow, he did not play the full 90 minutes for his country until nine internationals later. Kept out by combinations of Woodcock, Trevor Francis, Mark Hateley, Paul Mariner, Clive Allen, Peter Withe and Luther Blissett, Lineker had to wait until 26 March, 1985 for the complete item. It came in a 2–1 victory over the Republic of Ireland at Wembley. Needless to say, he scored. His first goal for England, from an opening made by new cap Peter Davenport 14 minutes from the end, proved to be the winner, since Liam Brady reduced the deficit just before the final whistle.

Even so, Lineker still had to be patient. Francis kept him out of the England team until the summer tour game against West Germany in Mexico City on 12 June, 1985. It was a notable occasion if only because England won 3–0, their biggest victory over the Germans for 50 years. The triumph may have been diminished by the knowledge that the Germans, foolishly, had given themselves only 48 hours to acclimatise to Mexico's thin air, but there was no denying the effectiveness of England's new striking partnership between Kerry Dixon and Gary Lineker. Dixon, then with Chelsea, scored twice against the Germans, and twice more in a 5–0 victory over the USA a few days later as the England bandwagon rolled on to Los Angeles. Lineker also helped himself to a couple of goals during the Californian scoring spree against a team of American students and indoor professionals. The quality of the opposition notwithstanding, that friendly proved to be the start of something big for him.

The following season, 1985–86, Lineker missed only three of England's 14 fixtures as they qualified for the finals of the World Cup and reached the last eight of the competition. An Everton player by then, he recorded his first international hat-trick in the 5–0 World Cup qualifying victory over Turkey at Wembley on 16 October, 1985. It meant that he scored six goals in his first 11 full games for England, a ratio of more than one every two games he kept up right to the end of his 80-cap career. Even so, he was not finding the target as regularly at that point as he became famous for later.

The hat-trick against the Turks represented Lineker's only contribution to England's qualifying campaign. Bryan Robson, with five goals, and Mark Hateley, with four, led the way as the unbeaten English booked their place in the Mexican finals of the 1986 tournament by finishing top of Europe's Group Three ahead of Northern Ireland, Romania, Finland and Turkey. Nor did Lineker score in the warm-up games against the former USSR in Tbilisi and against Canada in Vancouver. Worse still, the striker damaged his left wrist in a heavy fall against a Canadian defence of the lumberjack variety. For an anxious few hours, it looked as though the injury would put him out of the World Cup finals; but his – and Bobby Robson's – luck held when hospital examination revealed a severe sprain, not a fracture. To have lost his main striker then would have been a terrible blow for the England manager, since Bryan Robson's dislocated shoulder had popped out again during the warm-up match against Mexico in Los Angeles immediately prior to the game in Canada – an uncomfortable fact Bobby Robson kept secret until much later.

Playing on with his wrist heavily strapped, Lineker remained goalless as England began the World Cup finals disastrously in Monterrey by losing 1–0 to Portugal and drawing 0–0 with Morocco. Not only that, but they lost their two most experienced and influential midfield players, Bryan Robson and Ray Wilkins, in what seemed a catastrophic seven minutes before the interval of the match against Morocco. First, Robson fell awkwardly and put his troublesome shoulder out yet again, an injury that was to terminate his World Cup. Then Wilkins, normally a model of good sense, gained the unwanted distinction of becoming the first Englishman to be sent off in the finals of this competition. His offence was to throw the ball disgustedly towards the Paraguayan referee, Gabriel Gonzalez, after disputing an offside decision. Señor Gonzalez interpreted Wilkins's reaction as dissent and, having booked him earlier for obstruction, had no alternative but to send him off, a decision that was to cost the player a two-match suspension.

Thus, England could hardly be said to be overflowing with good cheer when they lined up against Poland five days later for a make-or-break match in Group F. Deprived of Bryan Robson and Wilkins, Bobby Robson brought Steve Hodge and Peter Reid into the midfield; but he also made other significant changes. Trevor Steven replaced Chris Waddle as the one genuine wide player in the team and, crucially, the clever little Peter Beardsley was preferred to Hateley, a more traditional type of English striker, alongside Lineker in attack. The last of those changes renewed a partnership tried only once before – in the 1–0 warm-up victory over the Soviet Union three months earlier. It had looked full of promise then, and now it positively brimmed over with good things.

After only eight minutes, Lineker and Beardsley began a swift, concerted attack that saw Lineker dart in front of his marker on the six-yard line to flash home a dipping centre from his then Everton colleague, Gary Stevens, on the right. Six minutes later, it was 2–0. Again Beardsley played a pivotal role, this time by changing the point of attack with a brilliant first-time pass out to Hodge on the left. When Hodge made ground and delivered the perfect centre, Lineker was running in to meet it with a killing shot. The Poles, who had drawn 0–0 with Morocco and beaten Portugal 1–0, could not believe what had hit them. Their goalkeeper, Mlynarczyk, must have been a bit shell-shocked by the time, late in the first-half, he let a corner by Steven slip through his hands. Needless to say, the England player who chested the gift down and slammed it high into the net was none other than Gary Lineker, suddenly as much a devastating match-winner for his country as for his club.

It is impossible to overestimate the value of that three-goal performance. It turned the tide for England, of course, and sent them on into the later stages of the 1986 World Cup; but it was also a watershed in Lineker's career. If one match can make a player, it was this one against Poland in his case. For the first time, it became clear that what he had been doing regularly against English defences, he was quite capable of doing against the more sophisticated Continental variety. The player himself readily acknowledges the influence that World Cup and that match had on his career. Asked, shortly before the finals of the 1992 European Championship, what his outstanding memories had been, Lineker said, 'Certainly the World Cups – they are the big thing. They stand head and shoulders above everything else. It's the limelight and everything, the importance of the event. They've been good to me, the two World Cups (he played in the 1990 finals as well, of course), and I'd have to remember Mexico particularly, because I finished top scorer. It was important to my career at that stage. It really took me a huge step forward from where I was. I ended up at Barcelona after that. If I had to single out one thing, it would be that World Cup; and if it had to be one game, it would be the one against Poland in Monterrey.'

Altogether, Lineker and Beardsley played as an attacking partnership for England 29 times. Its effectiveness and its essence is demonstrated clearly by the fact that Lineker scored 25 of his 48 international goals in those games, while Beardsley contributed only six. This was a true blend of armourer and marksman, as Lineker has readily acknowleged – with a codicil. 'People talk about partnerships, but it doesn't quite work like that at international level,' he says. 'In a way, it's obviously about the team performance: strikers haven't got a chance unless the team is playing well, because you've got to have the service. But international football is really an individual contest against your marker and the sweeper. You are not playing off another striker. You don't play like a lot of club sides do, where you knock it up and there's a big fellow flicking it on. It just doesn't work like that at international level.

'It is said that Peter Beardsley and myself made a good partnership, and I think the records prove it was prolific. That was because

Peter came to terms with playing very well in international football, and I continued to score the goals. We complemented each other because our strengths were totally different. He used to drop deep and take defenders out of the way. He is very aware like that. He'd get the ball outside the area and cause a lot of problems for defenders. That left the box free for me, which is the way I often like it. Sometimes, your own team-mates can take up the space. It wasn't an orthodox partnership, but it worked. England partnerships are very much an individual thing, and the one that is successful will be between the two players who adapt best to international football.'

Beardsley himself talks of Lineker in reverential tones. They may be good friends who used to room together and still socialise occasionally, but there is no mistaking the touch of awe in the Everton (and former Liverpool) striker's voice when he talks about the ability of his England partner. 'Gary's the best striker I've played with, and one of the best in the world,' says Beardsley with feeling. 'He's probably the most relaxed finisher I've ever played with, and I've played with some good ones. John Aldridge was a great finisher and Rushie [Ian Rush] was brilliant. I was also lucky enough to play with Clive Allen in one game for England. But Gary has proved time and time again how special he is.

'The unusual thing about him is that he doesn't always blast his goals in. A lot of good strikers hit the ball as hard as they can, but he always aims for the corners and usually sidefoots them in. That's the highest of qualities, and one not many people have got. Marco Van Basten, I'd say, is one of the few others who have got it. A lot of it is close stuff, but he's so aware of what's around him that he's able to take the slightest chance. One of the good things about Gary is that he appreciates what people do for him. He's been very good to me, but he doesn't have to be. He's the one that bangs the goals in, and it's a pleasure for me to play with him. You know he's always going to be there if you give him the chances.

'Our partnership worked well because he's a goalscorer and I'm more of a link-man. That's always been my game – to help the main striker. It's nice to score goals yourself, but it's never particularly bothered me who scores them, as long as someone does. That was what was good for me in 1986. People said I was doing very well, but if Gary hadn't scored those six goals nobody would have mentioned me. In a negative sort of way, it was lucky England's first two games didn't go so well. Bobby Robson had to make changes and, when he did, I got a chance and Gary scored a hat-trick. I was only involved in one of the hat-trick goals, really. People say it was all down to me, but he did brilliantly to score a hat-trick in a World Cup game.'

From Monterrey onwards, Lineker scored goals for England with the freedom of a man who had suddenly begun to believe in himself. He got two of the three against Paraguay that pitted his country, fatefully, against Argentina in the quarter-finals, and he claimed England's single strike as they went down 2–1 to Diego Maradona's infamous 'Hand of God' goal and the wayward little genius's breathtaking solo effort. Then, the following February in Madrid (by which time he was a Barcelona player), Lineker claimed all of England's goals as they beat Spain 4–2 in one of their most authoritative performances under Bobby Robson.

'I think Gary had just four chances that day, and he buried all four,' recalls the former England manager. 'They weren't easy chances, either: it was finishing of the highest calibre. I remember one particular strike with his left foot coming across an angled ball Beardsley put in. It was difficult because he had to change feet, it was on his left side and the defender was coming at him. He had about one second to make up his mind, change feet and hit it with his left foot, which he did. It went across the keeper and into the net. It was very similar to the shot he scored against Germany in the 1990 World Cup finals – the equalising goal.

'Everybody thought he was all right foot, but if it fell on his left he was not averse now and again to knocking it in. [Well done, Barry Lineker!] I remember that goal in Madrid because I thought to myself, "Christ, that is some finish!" That was a good night for him: four in one game against a team of high calibre and away from home. At the time, it was a pretty good Spanish team; but it was also absolutely brilliant finishing. I'll never forget it because it was also my birthday – 18 February.'

Robson has other treasured memories of the striker he probably understood as well as, if not better than, the eight other managers under whom Lineker served. 'I think one of the best games Gary ever played for England,' he says, 'was when we beat Poland 3–0 at Wembley in a World Cup qualifying match in early June 1989. That day, he led the line: he wasn't just a goalscorer. He worked to get into good positions to receive the ball. He knocked good balls back into midfield and he spun. If the full-backs, Kenny Sansom or Gary Stevens, had the ball in deep defensive positions, he'd make good runs across the defender so they could hit the ball over the top of the midfield into him. From there, he'd bring the midfield into play. He led the line that day in a way I'd never seen him do before. He was always lethal, and he was always going to score goals as long as he got the service, but on that particular occasion he played a very, very good, all-round game.'

Nevertheless, for all of Lineker's outstanding selflessness in that game against Holland, it is his inspired selfishness around goal that most people remember, Bobby Robson included. 'He had to rely on service,' admits the former England manager. 'He had to rely on other people round him to do things. He used to keep his fitness and his energy for finishing off the work of others. He didn't like chasing people when an attack broke down. He liked to hover and lurk and just be on the onside-offside of a defender. In many ways, he was a bit like Jimmy Greaves. People used to say Jimmy was lazy, but he was trying to keep just onside. With his pace – and Lineker was just the same – he could beat the offside trap; and once he got into space nobody could catch him. Gary was always ice-cool: he could always keep a cool head when he was going in on goal, and Jimmy Greaves was the same. I played with Jimmy, so I know how similar they were.

'What I liked about Gary – I think strikers are a special breed – was that he always wanted the ball into space. You get a lot of players who always want it deep. They come into you, away from the centre-half; but Gary was the opposite. He'd maybe come a yard, but then he'd spin and want the ball behind defenders and through defenders. He was a joy to play with. If I'd played with Gary Lineker as a midfielder, I know I'd have enjoyed it because I know where he'd have wanted the ball. He was not always coming to you for it to feet, he was always going away from you. Therefore he always gave you the opportunity of hitting the dream pass, the speculative pass into space. There aren't many players in the modern game who want the ball in that area – in other words, where it hurts the defender. He always did. He knew where it hurt the defender and that was the run he always wanted to make.

'One of the greatest goals he ever scored was against Holland when we drew 2–2 with them at Wembley shortly before the finals of the 1988 European Championship. I think they scored first – shocked us – and Gary Stevens hit a ball from right back between the left-back and down Van Tiggelen's side. It must have been a 40- or 45-yard pass, and Gary got on to it at full pelt. He spun on the centre-half, went through the gap and, as Van Breukelen came out to narrow the angle, he belted the ball through the goalkeeper and past him with ferocious pace. It was one of the best goals I've ever seen in my life.'

The European Championship finals that followed were not Lineker's, or Robson's, finest hour, of course. Having dropped only one point in the qualifying tournament, and run up a goal difference of 19–1, England went to West Germany as one of the favourites. However, they had peaked too early. Poor finishing and defensive errors led to a 1–0 defeat by the Republic of Ireland in the opening match, and that was followed by successive 3–1 defeats by Holland and the USSR. Lineker did not score a single goal this time and was conspicuous only for his lack of energy. The reason soon became apparent. A few days after England had gone out of the tournament, the striker was in hospital being treated for hepatitis.

'The '88 tournament was a big disappointment,' Lineker has admitted. 'We played quite well actually against the Irish but, myself included, missed a few chances. After that we were under pressure. Then we played a very good Holland side and got beat. It ended up in big disappointment because our confidence was so low by the time we played the USSR in the final game, we were awful. It was not a happy time from a personal point of view, either, since it was there I discovered I had hepatitis.'

He was not well enough to play in the first international of the following season, 1988–89, a friendly against Denmark at Wembley, but did recover in time for England's first qualifying match for the 1990 World Cup, a goalless draw with Sweden at home in October 1988. From that unpromising beginning, England did sufficiently well to qualify for Italia '90 by finishing second in their group, one point behind Sweden and four ahead of Poland. Poor Albania came bottom without a point to their name. Between his return in October 1988, and the controversial ending to his international career in the 1992 European Championship finals, Lineker missed only four of England's 49 matches and scored 22 goals.

At the World Cup finals in Italy, England again found themselves up against the Republic of Ireland and Holland, two of the teams who had turfed them out of the European Championship finals two years earlier. This time, though, the English were less tired because their First Division had been reduced by two to 20 clubs and the players had been given some breathing space. In addition, Paul Gascoigne had arrived on the scene and David Platt was about to join him among the ranks of world-class footballers.

Even so, England failed to beat either the Irish or the Dutch. An early Lineker goal against the Republic was cancelled out late on by Kevin Sheedy, and the second game was goalless. However, a 1–0 win aginst heroic Egypt, who had held both the Republic and Holland to a draw, was enough to put England into the first knock-out round, where they played Belgium in Bologna.

That, of course, was the game in which Platt, on as 71st-minute substitute for Steve McMahon, volleyed a memorable winning goal from a Gascoigne free-kick when a tight, absorbing contest was only seconds away from a penalty shoot-out. Lineker, not for the want of trying, had now gone three matches without a goal, but his barren spell was about to end dramatically in the quarter-finals.

The opponents were Cameroon, an emergent African nation so ebullient and self-confident that they looked quite capable of making even more history by going all the way to the final itself. Platt's headed goal put England in control after 25 minutes, but the second-half arrival of Cameroon's secret weapon, the 38-year-old striker Roger Milla, transformed the match. Having won a penalty, converted by Kunde after 61 minutes, Milla also delivered the pass from which Ekeke put the Africans ahead four minutes later.

Enter Gary Lineker to win the match for England off his own bat, as it were. Twice he was fouled as he went for goal, and twice he put the penalty-kicks away himself under intense psychological pressure. If any further proof were needed of his cool head and steady nerve, that rousing semi-final in Naples provided it. Lineker's equaliser came seven minutes from the end, and he scored the winner from the spot 15 minutes into extra-time. 'He said later he'd been thinking of his brother, Wayne, in Tenerife,' reported Bobby Robson, a little incredulously, of the first penalty.

So, England were in the semi-finals of the World Cup for the first time since they had won the trophy in 1966 by beating West Germany at Wembley. As luck would have it, their opponents in Turin were again the Germans, playing for the last time as one half of their country and strongly fancied to win the tournament after beating Yugoslavia, the United Arab Emirates, Holland and Czechoslovakia on their way to the last four. Yet, in the end, there proved to be only a couple of missed penalties between the old enemies. They slugged it out thrillingly right up to the end of extra time without a winner emerging. Andreas Brehme's rather fortunate free-kick goal for West Germany after 59 minutes, which looped crazily off Paul Parker and over Peter Shilton, was cancelled out ten minutes from the end of normal time by Lineker. All his predatory instincts served him well as three German defenders, Kohler, Augenthaler and Berthold, did a passable imitation of the Keystone Cops and he punished their laxity with a killing, left-footed shot. Both teams hit a post in extra-time, but neither could get the goal that would have rescued a noble contest from the indignity of a penalty shoot-out. Lineker got it off to a scoring start for England, and it was level-pegging at 3–3 when Stuart Pearce stepped forward to take the crucial fourth penalty for which Bobby Robson had saved him. 'If I had had to back one player,' said the England manager in his autobiography, 'it would have been Pearce, cool and with the hardest shot in the business. But Illgner saves with his feet and our world caves in. Pearce is distraught. What an unfair burden this is to put on an individual in a team sport.' Worse was to follow, Chris Waddle failing even to hit the target after Olaf Thon had given West Germany a decisive 4–3 lead from the spot. So, for the second World Cup running, England and Lineker had to cope with the disappointment of falling at one of the final hurdles.

Had he but known it, that heart-breaking defeat by West Germany was probably the pinnacle of his England career. At 29, Lineker was still in his prime – quick, alert, experienced and lethal. There were still one or two stirring moments to come at this, the highest level of the game, but any glory was confined to his involvement at club level with Tottenham. Over the last two years of his career in England, the beginnings of a decline from Lineker's physical peak were accompanied by the gradual and unexpected deterioration of his relationship with Graham Taylor, the England manager who had begun his reign by making the striker his captain and standard-bearer. The culmination of this unhappy set of circumstances was the *cause célèbre* of Lineker's substitution by Taylor in what proved to be the player's last appearance for England. But more of that later.

For the moment, let us dwell on Robson's final, glowing tribute to the striker he had plucked from obscurity: 'For a little feller, he was quite good in the air, you know. He wasn't like Mick Harford – he couldn't outjump big centre-halves – but he did have a certain ability in the air. He couldn't climb eight feet and head the ball, but he got some decent little goals for us with headers.

'He was a great player, but I never wanted him to think he could do things he couldn't. I used to say: "Keep it simple. Make a run, get on the ball. If you are in trouble, knock it off to somebody." We used to encourage people to get up to him so he could find somebody to play the ball off to. Then he would go again on the second run. He always had the energy to do that because he didn't chase full-backs or centre-halves. He was always fresh in his work. Therefore, he could make one run to hold it up, or he could make a decoy run, and he always had the energy to make another one as well. Sometimes, his second runs were brilliant.

'Although he wasn't the best of trainers, he still did it on the pitch because he had no weight problems. He looked after himself, he rested when he should, he kept his diet right, he kept his weight down, he was always trim. He was a model professional in that sense. He kept himself in fighting trim and he always had his pace. I don't know what percentage of his goals were down to his pace, but it must have been a lot.

'His second speed was his brain. He was very quick to see goal-scoring opportunities. He just seemed to know where the ball was going to go or fall. He had a really lively brain in the box, and that was a tremendous asset. He could always read it, he was always prepared for it.

'The one thing about Gary Lineker – and I think Graham [Taylor] would support this – was that there might be times when he did not play well, but he never hid. He never went behind defenders to hide. He was always wanting to play and looking to get in. I'm not saying he would hold the ball up right every time, or that he wouldn't miscue sometimes, but he was never guilty of not looking for opponents. That's why, I suppose, he was always very much in my mind.

'He was the guy who was going to put the ball in the net – off a rebound, off a goalkeeping mistake, off a bad back-pass, off a clever pass by one of us, off a good early cross in. He's going to be there, he's going to hunt. He was a hunter: he hunted off mistakes and good play. Mistakes occur at international level, just as they do in League football, because there's pressure on defenders. If there was a mistake in the box, he flashed on to it.

'Quite simply, he was as good as anyone I'd seen in that position. In terms of just finishing, he is the best I've seen or played with. He was a great boy to work with and a good professional. People liked him in the team because you always felt with Gary that if we played well he'd knock it in, and if we played not so well he'd still get a goal for us somehow at a critical time. I don't think you can go to places like Russia and Yugoslavia at international level and get the goals he did if you didn't have something special about you: and he was special.'

· 9 ·

England – The Agony

Jon Holmes still remembers the moment with some disbelief. 'I was sitting next to Michelle and she said: "They've taken Gary off!" And I said: "No, hold on a minute. I can't believe this!"' It was a common and widespread reaction to the substitution of Gary Lineker by England manager Graham Taylor, in the striker's last match for his country, his last chance to equal or break Bobby Charlton's 49-goal scoring record. By sending on Alan Smith, ironically Lineker's old attacking partner from the Leicester days, to replace him 27 minutes from the end of the European Championship game against Sweden in Stockholm on 17 June, 1992, Taylor succeeded only in bringing down the wrath of the English nation on his own head. The change had no material effect on the pattern of the game or its result, a decisive 2–1 win for the host country, but Taylor soon learned what it was like to be vilified on a grand scale. The defeat put England out of the finals much earlier than had been expected, and newspaper criticism of the manager the following day was predictably vicious. The *Sun*'s classic headline, 'Swedes 2, Turnips 1', was only the foliage on this particular vegetable patch.

The events of that game were the climax of one of the sadder episodes in the recent history of English football. No two men had seemed better suited than Taylor and Lineker to be manager and captain of England. Honest, approachable and good communicators, they looked to be a dream ticket from the moment Taylor made the appointment of Lineker one of his first acts on taking over from Bobby Robson as manager in the late summer of 1990. 'I felt,' says Holmes, 'when Taylor was made manager, he was perfect for Gary. I told him that what Taylor wanted of an England captain is what he could do. And it is fair to say that Gary wanted to be captain. He got the job, and we felt he was doing it according to what Taylor would want. But it was all weird. I don't know now why he made him captain in the first place.'

The decision was queried at the time because Lineker did not seem a natural leader and was playing in a position where it was difficult to rouse or support other players. Taylor explains it by saying: 'When I took over in 1990, England had just reached the semi-finals of the World Cup, but football had suffered terribly in the previous decade. Of the three people who had captained England, Peter Shilton and Terry Butcher had retired straight away and Bryan Robson was injured. Looking at the squad, there wasn't a captain in their mould: there just wasn't that kind of person available. What there was was this fellow Gary Lineker. He represented everything you wanted football to be represented by at that difficult time for the game. He had a very good image and he handled the press very articulately – something I consider important in an England captain. He also had an opportunity to break Bobby Charlton's scoring record, which I confidently expected him to do over the next two years.'

Yet, over that period, the relationship between Taylor and Lineker was to suffer a steady and irreversible decline. Although Taylor insists there was no real problem between himself and Lineker, relations had become so strained towards the end that they were sniping at each other through the press. Whose fault it was depends on your point of view and your interpretation of the evidence, which encompasses the controversial role of the agent in modern football and the increasingly complex relationship between players, managers, agents and the press.

'We felt all along that Taylor was testing Gary,' admits Holmes. 'For that reason, Gary begged me not to tell anyone in advance when he was made captain of England. So nobody knew. They didn't even know in my own office. Irving Scholar, chairman of Tottenham at the time, rang me one day and said: "Do you think he'll be captain?" I said I didn't know. We kept it absolutely secret and did everything by the book with Graham. The same thing happened when he told Gary he was going to drop Paul Gascoigne for the game against the Republic of Ireland in Dublin. We didn't tell a soul.

'I kept saying to Gary: "I think he's all right." But Gary said, "I don't know. There's something I'm not sure about." To be fair, Gary spotted it quicker than I did. Players see different things, of course. He saw him in stressful situations, whereas I was seeing him in situations where he'd clearly got a prepared brief.'

Even so, Holmes says he saw the final rift between Taylor and Lineker coming from a long way off. 'What happened in Stockholm was predictable. It has to be said that I felt there was something going wrong with the relationship when journalists were ringing me up and saying, off the record, that Gary wasn't going to be captain after the Republic of Ireland game [at Wembley on 27 March, 1991]. Taylor did pick him as captain again, much to our surprise, but I began to think there was something funny going on. Then I was told Taylor had said it would be nice if Gary went into the finals of the European Championship one goal short of the record. I said: "Taylor seems to have some problem with that." Gary never really worried about the record too much: he felt that if it came, it came. I thought: "He's messing about with him; he's trying to play games with him!" It went on and on, and I said to one or two people during the season: "There's some jealousy there, or something like that."'

What had sparked off that opening spat was Taylor's decision to reinstate Bryan Robson as captain on the Manchester United midfielder's return from the Achilles tendon injury that had caused him to be invalided out of the 1990 World Cup finals. Robson captained the side against Cameroon and the Republic of Ireland before succumbing once more to injury and bowing out of international football finally after one further appearance for England, against Turkey at Wembley on 16 October, 1991.

'When I brought Lineker back as captain,' says Taylor, 'I was invited out to lunch by Jon Holmes and asked why I had made Robson captain. But what was it to do with him? I didn't see that as any of his business. Anyhow, I could see that giving Robson back the captaincy seemed to have upset the situation. At that time, I didn't know whether Bryan Robson was going to come back permanently or not; but I'd 'phoned Gary Lineker at home to tell him before the change was announced. I told him that, because Bryan had captained England so many times, he would be captain for that particular game [Cameroon] and then we would see how it went from there. Robson hadn't been available for the first two or three internationals after I took over, but he'd captained England for so many years that it seemed to me it was right he should be reinstated at that time.

'The lunch with Holmes was purely a social occasion, so when you are getting into the sort of situation created by his question, you start to worry. Jon can use the words jealousy and envy if he wants, but it's not a case of that: it's a question of who's in control of the situation. It's a problem these days for managers because the press now talk direct to agents. I personally had no problem at all with my relationship with Gary Lineker. Perhaps the problem was that the agent didn't like some of the decisions I made. The agent manipulates people in my profession and he manipulates people in your profession [the press]. But for the benefit of what? For the benefit of himself as well as his client.'

Both Holmes and Lineker deny the charges hotly. 'Taylor makes it sound as though I stormed into him and demanded to know why Bryan Robson was captain and not Gary,' says Holmes, 'but I never do things like that. It wouldn't have been a very intelligent way to have dealt with it, anyway. I certainly don't remember asking him that question, and I would certainly accept that it was none of my business. Appointing the England captain is entirely the manager's decision. But I do remember him referring to it. I think he said: "David Miller [*The Times*' chief sports writer] had a go at me for this." If he had a resentment about it, why didn't he say to me at the time: "You shouldn't be asking me that." He knew me well enough.'

Lineker dismisses Taylor's claims in stronger and more detailed terms. 'When Bryan Robson was put back into the side,' he says, 'I expected him to be captain. There was never any ill-feeling there so far as I was concerned. So I don't see why that's a problem at all. I'd played under Bryan for years, so it wasn't a problem to me. Graham did ring me, as he said, and I accepted his decision. I don't think I had any moan at all to him then, and I certainly had no moan behind his back – not even to Jon.

'I think it really started – if Graham's perfectly honest – when he had a dig at me about the Republic of Ireland game at Wembley, when I was a bit tired. I did a piece with one of the newspapers saying I was tired, which was possibly not the right way to do it. But I just said honestly that I felt tired in the game and had been feeling tired in one or two other games. Graham was obviously not happy about that and had a dig at me in the press, which I don't think is the way to do things.

'He's done it to Dave Seaman and Chris Waddle to my knowledge. That, for me, is something a manager shouldn't do. On the Continent, if managers do that, they get kicked out by the players. In Spain, I found, the manager wasn't allowed to have a dig at the players in the press. It was just not the done thing. I know managers use the press to try to get players to do certain things, but as far as I'm concerned the way to do it is face-to-face. A newspaper editor wouldn't dream of criticising one of his journalists in the paper, and the relationship between manager and player in my opinion is exactly the same.'

So strongly did Lineker object to that kind of attack, he decided to have it out with the England manager at the first opportunity. 'The next time the squad met, I had a chat with Graham and told him I thought what he had done was unfair. I said that if he had been unhappy about what I'd done, he should have told me to my face and I would have accepted it, no problem at all. What wasn't acceptable, I added, was being attacked through the press, particularly with those off-the-record quotes that always come back to players. It had been made known to me that he'd upset one or two of the players with his remarks in the press, and I just thought that, as captain of the side, I should say something to him at that point about those things. I don't know whether that aggravated him or not, but he accepted it as fair criticism when I complained about what he was doing. I always thought we got on OK, actually, until I kept hearing about behind-the-back comments to the press. I heard the first after the Ireland game, and that's when you begin to wonder.'

The next signpost pointing downhill in this relationship came in the form of England's summer tour. Inherited from the previous régime, it took them to Australia, New Zealand and Malaysia, a long way from home and largely uncharted territory in football terms. Predictably, a lot of the big clubs took one look at the exhausting itinerary and pulled their players out of the squad. Lineker, however, insisted on going despite the fact that his club, Tottenham, wanted him to accompany them on their tour of Japan. Some cynics felt the striker was simply looking for easy goals in his quest for Charlton's record; but Holmes insists his client felt that, as captain of England, he had a responsibility to the team, especially at a time when a lot of young players were being blooded. Taylor, incidentally, supports that interpretation of events. In the end, player and club arrived at a compromise, Lineker breaking off from the England tour in New Zealand to fly to Tokyo to play one game for Spurs (which they lost 4–0 and in which the England captain, not surprisingly, looked jet-lagged after a flight of more than ten hours from Wellington).

So where was the problem? 'Gary Lineker was very adamant and strong that he would come to play for England,' Taylor recalls. 'In fact, the information I received was that he was being very strong with Terry Venables because Tottenham had this tour to Japan. What was interesting was that, when Gary went to play for Tottenham in Japan, Jon Holmes should arrive there and that, not long afterwards, we were to hear that Gary Lineker was to go out and continue his career in Japan. Not only, therefore, did he come out of that situation looking as though he wanted to play for England, but he still got his game in Japan and, presumably, still got the negotiations going for his move to that country. Then, of course, he came back and scored all four goals against Malaysia!'

Taylor says he respects Lineker for that kind of comprehensive planning and efficiency, but the compliment seems forced. Especially when it is followed by: 'The point I am making about this is that here we have a man who is England captain, and when I made him captain he said he didn't want to look any further than the finals of the 1992 European Championship in Sweden. Yet, a year into his captaincy, he is in Japan looking for his future. In view of what Gary had said about retiring after Sweden, I looked at Alan Shearer and David Hirst in the game against France and made him substitute. I was hammered unmercifully for that, yet in Japan six months earlier – while England were still in New Zealand – he was in the first stages of his negotiations to continue beyond Sweden. I'm sure Gary Lineker wanted to play for England all of the time. The point I'm making about it is that he or his agent also saw a very good opportunity in terms of where there was some more money to be earned. And, in fact, they used the situation very well – club, country, what have you.'

Holmes readily admits the negotiations for Lineker's transfer to Grampus Eight were started in earnest in Tokyo that summer, but he insists there was nothing underhand or surreptitious about the arrangement. 'When the Japanese heard Gary would be in Tokyo for that match, they suggested a meeting,' he claims. 'That is why I went out there. If our only concern had been the negotiations with Grampus Eight, it would have been much simpler for Gary to have gone on the club tour to Japan with Spurs.' Lineker, for his part, makes the point that he was prepared to commit himself exclusively to England and agreed to make the quick trip to Japan only under pressure from others, including Taylor himself. 'Originally, I wasn't going to Japan,' he says, 'I was sticking by the England tour all the way. I'd had a few discussions with Terry Venables and eventually decided I was going to go with England. I told Graham that and he seemed very pleased I'd made the effort, because it's not always easy standing up to managers.

'Then we were at an England get-together not long before the tour, and he's called me into his office. 'There's a Japanese delegation coming,' he said. 'They are desperate for you to go on the Tottenham tour. If you don't go, there's a possibility they'll pull Tottenham out, and I'm under a lot of pressure to let you go.' I said that if he wanted me to stay with England, I was perfectly willing to go along with that. Then, sure enough, a Japanese delegation came to see Graham Taylor at Burnham Beeches Hotel [where the England squad live when they are training at the Bisham Abbey National Sports Centre in Berkshire] to try and persuade him to let me go to Japan. He and Lawrie McMenemy [Taylor's assistant] had a chat with me. They'd always said it was the England tour or nothing, so I repeated that if they really wanted me to stick out for the England tour, I'd do so. But Graham Taylor said: "We're under pressure; perhaps it wouldn't be a bad idea if you went and played one game and then came back to us in Malaysia.' I said I'd be prepared to do that for the club, but only if it had his [Taylor's] full go-ahead.

'What I was trying to do was accommodate everybody and do the right thing. That seemed to me like a very sensible compromise all round, although I was still disappointed at missing one of the England games. So that's exactly what happened. And once it was announced I was going to Tokyo, Grampus Eight – who we'd hardly heard anything of before – asked whether it would be possible to have a meeting in Japan. I agreed, but I didn't really think at that stage anything would come to fruition. Grampus Eight also asked Jon Holmes to go out. They flew him out separately just for a day or so. We met them, but it was only the first sort of informal talks.'

Lineker, who claims Taylor has never mentioned the subject before, expresses surprise that the England manager has waited so long to complain about the Japanese connection during that summer tour nearly two years ago. He also makes it clear that he kept Taylor fully informed of his plans to move into Japanese football, and was even prepared to sacrifice his lucrative move to Grampus Eight in the interests of England's European Championship campaign. 'I actually told him about the possibility of the move a long time before it became public – at least two months before,' reveals

Lineker. 'I think it was probably at the time of England's first friendly that season (1991–92). I told him, at the same time, I was definitely going to retire from international football at the end of the European Championship, regardless, and I was very up front with him about it. I said: "I'll tell you this: if you've got a problem with that, and it'll affect the rest of the season as regards England, I'll pull out of the Japanese thing." To which he actually said something like: "No, it wouldn't be a bad move for myself in the future." He also said my decision to retire was OK with him and didn't make any difference to the situation so far as he was concerned. But it seems to have got to him a little bit, and I don't know why.'

One thing Taylor does bridle at is Holmes's suggestion that he was jealous of Lineker's expertise at public relations. 'There's no need for me to be jealous or envious of those kind of things,' snorts the England manager. 'I can't see how he can justify saying it. If he felt that, he should have picked up the 'phone and said: "Look, what's all this problem about?" When he wanted Gary Lineker to be captain of England, he was very adept at picking the 'phone up and speaking to me about it. My relationship with Gary Lineker was all right so far as I was concerned.'

That is not how Holmes remembers it, however. 'I never rang him up asking him to make Gary captain,' states Lineker's agent. 'I must have been bloody adept because I don't remember doing it. In fact, I deny it completely. If you think about it, that would have been a fairly stupid thing to do. It's not the sort of question you ask because it's likely to be counter-productive. It surprises me Taylor consented to talk to me afterwards if I was ringing up and making that kind of impertinent call.'

One of the more intriguing aspects of the Taylor–Lineker conflict was why the manager, if he had such a good relationship with the player as he claims, appeared to keep chivvying him through the press in some kind of long-range geeing-up process. 'I think the thing is that other people look to the captain to see what the captain's doing,' says Taylor, by way of an explanation. 'It's not so much the manager as the captain the other players are looking towards: seeing if he's out training, seeing if he's enthusiastic for training. As captain of England, he had a responsibility to come out on to the training pitch. I'm led to believe he didn't do it previously.' Again, one is bound to wonder why Taylor did make Lineker captain in the first place. His own words suggest he was aware of the striker's almost legendary lack of enthusiasm for conventional training.

Yet Lineker insists that he deliberately became a more conscientious trainer while he was captain of England. 'I made a conscious effort to improve my training under Graham Taylor,' he claims, 'because I knew it was important to him. Obviously, you want to create the right impression, and as captain I felt I ought to. I hardly missed a session and tried to be as enthusiastic as I could – probably more so than I'd been at any other time in my career. So it looks as though he is just pulling out various excuses, old ones at that.'

When, in February 1992, Lineker was left out of the Wembley team to play France, then favourites to win the European Championship, it caused a sensation. This was the first time he had been dropped since early in his England career, and the decision was made all the more remarkable by the spectacular and vitally important goal he had scored in the previous international, three months earlier. With England a goal down to Poland in Poznan and needing a draw to qualify for the finals of the European Championship, Lineker had volleyed an equaliser over his shoulder 13 minutes from the end. Taylor confessed that, as time ran out, he had been praying that a chance would fall to his most reliable goalscorer.

Not unreasonably, the England manager chose to see that goal as confirmation that – after two barren games – Lineker's scoring touch had returned and as an excuse to look at other striking options, beginning with Shearer, then of Southampton, and Sheffield Wednesday's Hirst. Lineker saw his omission rather differently, though. 'He [Taylor] told me the day before the game, and naturally I was disappointed,' says the player. 'I'd scored the winner in the previous game against Poland; this was a big game at Wembley; there were not going to be too many of them left for me; and I was really disappointed at being left out. Personally, I didn't think it was a fair decision, but I accepted it for what it was and for the reasons he gave; I could understand his argument to a degree. I've got no divine right to play, and if he wanted to leave me out that was his right: he's the England manager. My main objection was that he didn't give me any time to think about it. If he'd have rung me up the week before and said: 'I'm leaving you out and bringing these players in,' then we could have sorted out between us what we were going to say. But it was the day before, and it left me in a tricky position with the media.

'Even if he'd given me a bit more time, it wouldn't have been easy. Imagine doing a press conference straight after training and saying something emotional that I'd regret later. I would have only had to say I wasn't pleased with the decision, and you can imagine the headlines: "Lineker Slams Taylor". I had to make a quick decision on my own, and I decided to go back to the hotel, not answer the 'phone and just say nothing. Whatever I'd said would have been taken out of context. If I'd told the truth and said: "No, I'm not happy at being left out", the headlines would have gone berserk. And if I'd actually said I thought it was a good decision and it was up to him, that would have been lying – which, again, you don't want to do. It would also have looked a bit pathetic if I'd said: "Oh, it's a really good decision!" when I didn't think it was. So the only alternative I had, for the good of the manager, the team and me, was to keep quiet for a while. And, until now, I never have said anything about it.'

The vow of silence was a decision with which Holmes was in full agreement when Lineker contacted him. 'Gary rang me and was clearly quite upset about it,' reports his agent. 'It was not so much being left out that upset him as the timing of it. Taylor didn't tell him about it until the morning of the day before the match, and he felt that, as captain, he deserved more advance warning than that. Anyway, he asked my advice, and I said the best thing for us to do would be to say absolutely nothing. "Let's see what happens," I said, "but we'll say nothing. Anything you say is going to be misinterpreted."

'All I did all afternoon was play a completely straight bat to everyone. I kept on saying he was not saying anything to anyone. When journalists said: "Off the record, is he upset?" I replied: "Listen, that's up to you. But he's saying nothing." And, of course, all the press lads savaged Taylor in the papers the next day. It wasn't me who put them up to it at all. They decided that was what they wanted to write. Because no-one was giving any quotes, they had to say what they felt. Obviously, they read something in the situation. Then, the next day, at the post-match press conference, Taylor made some remark to the effect that Jon Holmes will be pleased because Lineker came on at half-time. I know Taylor and Lawrie McMenemy believed I'd stirred up all the press against them. But, honestly, I'm blameless on that.'

Taylor would not agree. 'I think,' he says pointedly, 'that Jon Holmes was adept at making sure Gary Lineker never said anything himself, but said it all for him. And I don't think that is the way to go about things. If there is any disagreement I would have with Jon Holmes, it is that – if you take the France game, there was no problem there; there was no question of Gary running away from anything at all. But certain journalists could then 'phone Jon Holmes and get all the quotes they wanted provided they were not putting Gary Lineker's name on them. There's no envy or jealousy in that. The England manager has to deal with a situation he's been put into by an agent because he doesn't want his client – be he the England captain or not – having quotes attributed directly to him. But why not? If there's anything that causes the problem, it's the agent.'

Needless to say, Holmes disagrees violently. 'He seems to attribute to me greater powers than I believe I have,' says Lineker's agent. 'If I had the powers he says I have, I'd probably be a lot richer and in much greater demand than is in fact the case. Journalism, in many ways, has got to such a state now that everybody believes everything is a quote and no journalist has an opinion of his own.'

Lineker backs Holmes up by adding: 'The next time we met, I actually told him [Taylor] why I didn't say anything to the press. What concerns me is the way he's now had a go at me for not saying anything to them on that occasion. As for this business about manipulating the press, as far as I'm concerned all I've ever done is just speak to them, given an honest opinion and – I'm quite famous for it – sat on the fence. I try to be careful what I say and I don't give off-the-record stuff: it's something I've never done. So I don't see how I manipulated the press: I shouldn't think good journalists could be manipulated, anyway. It's probably more of a dig at Jon than at me.'

Having come on in the second half against France, Lineker duly scored, of course. Indeed, Taylor saw the captain's lively performance as justification for having started with him on the bench. Shearer had already scored in the first half of his senior debut, and their two goals gave England a victory over the French that was to signal the beginning of the end of the glittering revival that country had enjoyed under the inspirational management of the charismatic Michel Platini. Lineker scored again in the game after next, a 2–2 draw with the CIS (the former USSR) in Moscow on 29 April, 1992, leaving him just one goal short of Charlton's 22-year-old record. He should have equalled it there and then, from Nigel Clough's through pass, but failed to beat the advancing goalkeeper when clear of the defence.

No matter, everyone thought, there are still three more warm-up games, against Hungary, Brazil and Finland, and a minimum of three matches in the European Championship for Gary to complete the formality of becoming the most prolific scorer in England's history. Little did we all know then that he had already scored his last goal for his country. There was just one more real chance. In the 1–1 draw with Brazil at Wembley on 17 May, 1992, Lineker won a penalty himself when he was brought down by the Brazilian goal-keeper, Carlos, as they vied for a long through pass to the right of goal. Taking the kick as England's tried and trusted penalty-taker, the ace marksman fluffed his shot for once and enabled Carlos to make an easy save.

It was after that friendly that Taylor took Lineker to task quite severely through the media. It began at the immediate post-match press conference when I, in all innocence, asked for the manager's opinion of the experimental attacking partnership between Lineker and David Platt. By way of a reply, he praised Platt's industry with an enthusiasm that left little doubt he was dissatisfied with Lineker's work-rate. 'If you look at the two up front,' said the England manager with feeling, 'I've got to be happy with Platt. He's had a lot of hard work to do. He got into good positions and he scored his goal.'

Subsequently, in an interview with two Sunday newspapers fol-lowing the announcement of the 20-man squad for Sweden, Taylor made his dissatisfaction with Lineker's performance even clearer. 'When somebody is almost a national institution,' said Taylor, 'it's almost as if you can't touch them. I'm not into all that. Looking at it realistically, we could perhaps argue that we played Brazil with ten men.'

Not surprisingly, those sort of sharply critical comments to the media did not go down very well with Lineker or Holmes. 'Then we got all that business after the Brazil game,' says Holmes. 'By chance, we found out about the Sunday stories in advance through a jour-nalist on one of the papers running the tale. We were told Taylor had had a right go at Gary, which didn't surprise him because he said the manager seemed to him to have been incredibly hyped-up and stressful after he'd had to pick the squad for the European Championship finals following the game against Brazil.

'Anyway, we thought about it, and I told Gary he should tackle Taylor about it. In the meantime, it just so happened that I had to ring Taylor about whether Gary could have a mobile 'phone when they went to their secluded training camp in Finland because of the situation with George [the Linekers' baby son, who had contracted leukaemia]. Taylor had gone on to the players about there being no 'phones, and he didn't want anyone to 'phone back, etc. etc. Having explained why Gary needed to keep in touch with Michelle, I said: "You two ought to have a chat, you know, because sometimes things can get out of hand." He replied that he didn't like to speak to Gary about the baby, but his explanation why didn't make an awful lot of sense to me.

'Gary did approach him personally on the Saturday night, told him he'd heard the story was coming out and put two specific quotes to him. But Taylor flatly denied it: flatly denied making any of those remarks. Well, we knew what was going to be in the papers the following day, and sure enough there it was. One of the journalists involved wrote in his piece something to the effect that he hoped Gary and Taylor wouldn't fall out because it was important for England that they didn't. That thought was echoed by most of the press the following day, when they asked what the hell was going on. When Gary went down to join England on the Tuesday, Taylor had him in and apologised. "I went over the top, and I'm completely out of order," he admitted. So I don't know what to make of that situation. Did the bloke forget he'd made the remarks? He seems to think everything is calculated, but I'm not sure it's quite as calculated as he believes. The whole thing was an odd sequence.'

Taylor challenges fiercely the claim that he denied saying what the Sunday papers eventually reported. 'That's a complete fabrication,' he retorts. 'What, in fact, I did do was contact one of the journalists concerned and get hold of his tape-recording to see exactly what it was I had said. When Gary Lineker came to me to complain that he'd been criticised by me and had heard one or two things, I actually held fire on that and said: "Look, I'm going to go back and see exactly what it is I have said." Then I did say to Lineker: "Yes, I did say these things," and I explained to him it came at the end of a very, very heavy day for me. It's not true that I apologised, in the sense that I had denied anything I'd said previously. What I did say to him was: 'It was the end of the day, and perhaps it would have been better if some of the things hadn't been said." The next thing I know, I'm reading in one paper that there's been a complete apology. Who gave that story out? It goes on and on.'

The answer to Taylor's pointed question, says Gary Lineker, is

Gary Lineker. 'The person who leaked it to the press that Graham apologised was me, not Jon Holmes as he seems to think. He seems to have a go at Jon just to try and have a back-handed go at me for some reason. When we arrived in Finland for the pre-tournament preparation just before the European Championship, I was asked by pressmen at the airport if the manager had apologised. I said that he had but I didn't want to go into it any more than that. "As far as I'm concerned," I said, "the matter is finished." That's where the papers got the story from. It wasn't an off-the-record comment; it was an on-the-record comment. So why he [Taylor] should now come out and deny he apologised, I don't know. He did offer those excuses, which I understood. I realised it was a difficult time picking a squad and leaving people out, and I also accepted his apologies for what they were. Now, for him to deny that is, for me, just not on.'

According to Lineker, the sequence of events that followed his premature discovery of Taylor's newspaper criticism of him was as follows: 'Brazil wasn't the best game I've ever had, although it wasn't the worst, either. I think it perhaps got to him [Taylor] that I'd missed the penalty. Anyway, I asked him about these things, and pointed out that it had been a bit upsetting to me. I asked him straight out – it doesn't matter what he says now – and he vehemently denied saying any of those things that eventually came out in the papers. He said he definitely didn't say anything like that, and didn't know where they had got it from. He said the only thing he'd said was that he thought, when asked about my performance, that Platt had done very well. So I threw the quote at him about playing with ten men, and he said there was no way in the world he would say anything like that. This was the day before the story appeared, I think – the Saturday. So he said: "I'll get the papers in the morning myself, and we'll see where we go from there."

'Obviously, it all came out, and the other papers picked it up the next day. A day or two later, we are flying out to Finland and are in the hotel at Heathrow. He [Taylor] called me in straight after we'd got there, saying he wanted to chat privately in his room. There was only him and me there. Again, regardless of what he says now, he did apologise. His first words were: "First of all, I must apologise." He said it had been an emotional day with the squad, etc., etc., and I accepted the apology. I thought it was big of him to make the apology and I was perfectly happy after that.'

Lineker hit the bar, but did not score against the Finns in Helsinki. Nor was he any more successful against Denmark and

France in England's first two games in the finals of the European Championship, both goalless draws. Worse still, he rarely looked like scoring. Either the chances had dried up, or he had lost his touch. Then again, there might have been other reasons. Holmes had felt, from England's arrival in Sweden, that things were not quite tickety-boo in the camp.

'Gary will talk himself into believing things are right because they have to be right,' says his agent. 'He was telling me things were all right when I could see clearly they were not. He appeared on television with Taylor the first day of the European Championship – that's when Taylor made that ludicrous remark to Elton Welsby: "It's none of your business!" or something – and my wife said to me: "Why is Gary trying to get off the edge of the screen?" Gary was leaning right away from Taylor, and the body-language said an enormous amount. But when I spoke to him, he continued to insist everything was all right. I felt he was just saying that because he needed to feel things were right: he couldn't have played properly if he had believed they were not.

'This is common among sportsmen. They will talk themselves into being in the right frame of mind. I can remember Will Carling when the England rugby team got stuffed by Australia on tour. I said to him: "That was a bit of a blow wasn't it?" But he replied: "No, I think it's done our boys good." He'd clearly rationalised it to himself, and they all do it. It's not a question of being dishonest with themselves: if they accepted the truth of the matter, they'd pack up.'

Whatever the state of his relationship with Lineker at that point, Taylor picked him for the final game in Group One, a severe test since England now had to beat Sweden in Stockholm to qualify for the final stages of the tournament. Everything went according to plan for 45 minutes. England, fielding their most attacking formation of the finals, led at the interval with the slightly streaky goal David Platt had scored, from a centre by Lineker, after only three minutes and were playing well enough to win against the odds.

The situation was transformed by Sweden's introduction of Johnny Ekström at the restart as a substitute for the disappointing Anders Limpar, of Arsenal. Ekström, tall, strong and quick, was pushed forward with Klas Ingesson, Martin Dahlin and Tomas Brolin to form a powerful, four-pronged attack. Suddenly, England could not cope with the pressure stoked up by quick, accurate Swedish service from midfield. The host nation equalised after 51 minutes in a thoroughly predictable manner, central defender Jan Eriksson coming forward to score with his head from a corner as he had in his country's opening match against France.

Then, as England continued to take a pounding, came the fateful moment when Taylor decided the situation could be improved by taking off Lineker and sending on Alan Smith. The manager's reasoning was that the team needed someone to hold the ball up in attack to stop the Swedes returning it to the England penalty area as soon as it was cleared by the English defence. However, it was an explanation that took some swallowing: it was questionable whether Smith was any better than Lineker at holding the ball up, and most observers felt that a more effective way of reducing the Swedish pressure would have been to strengthen the English midfield.

In any case, it seemed crazy to take off your most expert goalscorer, a man renowned for rescuing lost causes, at a time when the score was 1–1 and, mathematically at least, England were still in with a chance of winning. The effectiveness of the switch may be judged by the fact that England did not score again, but Sweden did. A wonderful goal it was, too, Brolin exchanging passes slickly with Dahlin before driving the ball past Chris Woods. Thus, when Taylor suggested, at the immediate post-match press conference, that Sweden had reminded him of the successful team he had had at Watford between 1977 and 1987, there was no shortage of incredulity.

Even so, Taylor continues to stick to his guns over the tactical justification for the substitution. 'It was made purely on football grounds,' he insists, 'and people are perfectly entitled to disagree with that if they so wish. I felt the game had gone away from us so much in the second half that we were under a great deal of pressure. When you are in that position, you need somebody at least to be able to get hold of the ball and make it stick to give you a little bit of a chance. People may say: "OK, we could have done something else and kept Gary on." Of course that's right, but I made that decision anyhow.

'What happened, amongst the emotion of it all, is that my plans were disrupted. It had been my intention to drop David Platt back into midfield for Neil Webb and bring on Alan Shearer as well up front. Unfortunately, Andy Sinton went over on his ankle and was brought off, so I sent on Paul Merson to take his place. Amongst all the emotion of Gary Lineker coming off, that change was never discussed. I felt the way things had gone, we needed more strength up front to get us back into the game.'

Significantly, however, the England manager confesses now that, with hindsight, he should not have taken Lineker off. But not for the obvious reasons. 'If I was a really political animal, and given the same set of circumstances,' he says, 'I'd leave him on – but not for purely footballing reasons. What it actually shows is that sometimes the substitution of a person like Gary Lineker goes beyond football matters. Therefore, when I say I would leave him on, I mean only if I was thinking of more than just football – which perhaps I should have been. Because it's given people so much ammunition, and it's not always ammunition that's fired at you straight on. It's the sniping that's the worse.'

So far as Holmes was concerned, the England manager was simply acting predictably. 'I suppose I wasn't completely surprised when Gary got taken off,' he says. 'I felt more sad and disappointed, in a way, because I always quite liked Taylor and thought he was quite good at his job. But he'll obviously have a problem talking to me now because I'm clearly one of the villains of the piece so far as he's concerned. This grating stuff about not being able to criticise Gary because he's a national hero: I suppose he'd blame me more for that than Gary. He's never asked me how I think he should handle the situation, though other managers have. But that's up to him. You do something you believe is good for the sport, and all you get from other quarters is jealousy because they are not quite as good at it as you are. You begin to wonder whether it's worth the effort.'

Later that night, Holmes telephoned Lineker at the England team hotel. 'Michelle had been over there and spoken to him, and she asked me to give him a ring on the mobile 'phone. We were just chatting, and I said: "It's a fuck-up, isn't it?" He agreed, adding: "Well, he [Taylor] got his own little say in, didn't he!" We both knew that what we had feared would happen had happened. We saw it coming from a long way off, and we were both being realistic.

'In retrospect, the whole thing amazes me. What Taylor did wasn't that clever anyway, because if he'd wanted to shaft Gary, he should have let him play to the end. Then he could have said: "Well, I gave him a chance, but I'm sorry he didn't get it [the scoring record].' His explanation for the substitution was complete nonsense – some rubbish about the long ball game and hanging on to

the thing. In my opinion he just made himself more and more fool-
ish. Really and truly, if you examine his decision, you would have to
ask him a lot of searching questions about what happened. It was
an incredibly bad decision if only because he enabled the press to
focus on it. When you get people like John Junor – who's never
written about football in his life – and Bernard Ingham slagging you
off, you know you must have put your foot in it.

It is a view that attracts widespread support even now. Qualifying, perhaps, as something of a neutral because he is Scottish,
Graeme Sharp, Lineker's old attacking partner at Everton, called
the substitution 'a scandalous decision'. He adds: 'No matter how
badly Gary's been playing, when the ball's in the six-yard box he's
dangerous. But he never got a chance in Sweden. He was up on his
own all the time. You'd never say Gary was great for his work-rate,
closing people down or anything. That's not his game; but when
he's in the box, he's tireless.'

Terry Venables, the man who signed Lineker for Barcelona and
for Tottenham, delivers a similar verdict in a different, more diplomatic way. 'If you've got Gary in your team,' he says, 'I believe you
go with him or you don't. He's always liable – like in Poland – to
score the vital goal. If you don't like his style of play, don't play
him. But if you do play him, you've got to go right the way through
with it. Taking him off, as Graham Taylor did, is not something I
would have done. That's all I would say. That doesn't make it right.
You know before the game Gary's not going to do certain things:
it's not something you discover after 70 minutes. You cannot be a
little bit pregnant: you are either supportive or you're not.'

Bobby Robson, the manager who brought Lineker into the
England team, was reluctant to become involved in the debate. The
target, while in office, for hurtful criticism by one of his own predecessors, Robson did not want to be accused of the same sniping
himself. Even so, he could not help admitting of the substitution:
'I'd have to say, yes, I was surprised when Graham took him off. I
wondered about the deliberation of it.' For the most part, Robson
would talk only about his period in charge of the national team; but
that was critical enough in its way.

'I can't say how Graham felt at the time because it was two years
later and things might have changed,' said his immediate predecessor, 'but when I was manager I don't think I was ever in a
position where I could afford to take Lineker off: I always felt he
would get a goal even if it was the last minute. You always felt like

keeping him on because he might nick one. He was too dangerous to take off.

'All right, he's not playing well, he's lost the ball, he's missed a chance, he's not looking so sharp today, etc., etc., but I always felt with Gary Lineker that if you played him for the whole game he might get you a goal in the 59th second of the last minute. For me, it would always be a risk to take him off – particularly if you were looking for a goal. If anybody in the side was going to get it, he was the one most likely to chalk. I believed in him but, two years later, Graham might have felt differently about it.'

Robson also puts a new slant on the accusation, made by Taylor, that Lineker was not holding the ball up sufficiently against the Swedes. 'It may be true that he doesn't hold the ball up well sometimes,' says Robson, 'but when he played with Peter Beardsley, the little fella was a good foil for him. Beardsley had instant touch, and Beardsley could hold it up. We could play the ball into Beardsley, then on to Lineker. So when they had that good combination, that part of Lineker's game didn't disturb us too much. In Sweden, he didn't have anybody to play off: I saw that myself. Nobody made a chance for him, did they?'

Sadly, Beardsley did not make it to Sweden. Nor did Chris Waddle, another 'flair' player who fell out with Taylor. Then there was the absence through injury of both Paul Gascoigne and John Barnes. Yet Taylor insists that no effort was spared to make sure Lineker had the bullets to fire. 'Gary Lineker's a goalscorer,' concedes the England manager. 'I might even have christened him the King of the Penalty Box myself. During the two years I was in charge of England and Gary was captain, I was regularly making demands of the team to try to get the ball into positions so that Gary Lineker could put it into the net. One of the things we were in full agreement on was that England should get the ball forward into the box more quickly, particularly for people such as him, because that is where he worked.

'If you look at the records, I think you'll find that Gary scored more than a goal every two games for me [it was 13 goals in 22 appearances], which was as good as it had been previously. The chances were always there. I think he would be the first to admit he didn't have the best of European Championships. In the summer, when he was scoring goals on the tour, I made the point that if you took a photograph of Gary putting the ball away, invariably someone like David Platt would be in the picture. David went a year without scoring a goal, but suddenly he claimed all five England had scored in seven games. If you took photographs of his goals, you'd probably find Lineker was in them. The chances were being created and, originally, Lineker was getting to them; but in that last little spell, someone else was getting there first.'

Quite obviously, Taylor had come to the conclusion that, at nearly 32, England's leading goalscorer was not the international force he had been. 'There were people who were already suggesting before the European Championship finals that Gary had not been performing for a little bit,' argues the England manager. 'He'd had a lot of personal problems, hadn't he, with the child and all of those sorts of things going on. There are people who believe I should have made a decision about him much earlier than half an hour from the end of our third game in the finals. That I didn't do that, I think, shows how supportive I was, in fact.'

Indeed, Taylor is on record as saying that the substitution ought to have been made in the previous match. 'With hindsight,' he told the *Sunday Times*' football correspondent, Tony Francis, 'perhaps I should have substituted him against France. He had only one shot at goal. Against Denmark, I don't remember any. Gary will admit he had not been as sharp as we'd have liked. In training, his shots were hitting the bar or rebounding off the goalkeeper. I got it into my head that he was in a rut.'

And what of the most important witness of all, Gary Lineker himself? What did he think about the substitution? Up to now, he has kept his own counsel and studiously avoided becoming involved in the controversy. But Taylor's criticism of him in this chapter triggered off a sudden outpouring of all those suppressed feelings. Not that what he has to say is pure vitriol, by any means. Typically, his view of the incident is delivered with the objectivity, emotional restraint and good humour for which he has become famous. Nevertheless, there is a sharper cutting edge than usual to some of the words.

'It was very disappointing at the time,' he admits, beginning in a typically non-commital way, 'but it was everybody else who went overboard about the substitution, not me. It was a game of football and I was brought off. To be perfectly honest, if I'd stayed on it's unlikely I would have scored because we were really up against it at the time. The fact that I was brought off in the last game didn't bother me too much. The only thing was, I just fancied I might get one. I probably wouldn't have done, but I just fancied I might.

'The [England scoring] record doesn't matter to me. In fact, just think of all the years of freedom I'll get now from people saying: "Are you worried about your record being broken?" Poor old Bob is going to have that for another 20 years. I'm perfectly happy to have done what I've done. Of course I'd have liked to score a few more goals; of course I'd have liked to win the European Championship. But how can I complain about what's happened in my career?

'The European Championship wasn't the greatest tournament for me, but strikers usually suffer when the team's not playing well. Having said that, I hold up my hands and admit it wasn't the best I've played, either. The funny thing is, in that one particular game against Sweden, it was the best I'd felt in the whole tournament. I had a hand in our goal and, with a bit of luck, could have had a break. I was quite pleased in that game, particularly the first half, when I thought we played really well.

'The substitution, for me, is just a decision that was up to the manager. Other people said they thought it might be a personal thing, but I never really believed that until I heard some of the things he [Taylor] has come out with. Now, you think, perhaps it was. This may be unfair, I don't know, but it seems to me that after he's made the decision to pull me off, he's looked back and decided on different reasons for things over the years to stir up something in our relationship. It's as if he's got to justify it somehow. I don't know why he felt he had to do that. Only he knows, really. It's gone: he got stick for it, but that's not my fault. So what's his problem? Then again, I shan't worry unduly about it. I've got far more important things to worry about.'

Taylor, in point of fact, indicates that he has left a lot about the Lineker affair unsaid since he believes there has to be a degree of confidentiality and trust between managers and players, and between players and players. 'When professional footballers are together,' says the England manager, 'they must have a confidence and trust in one another because none of us is perfect. I've never believed in going and blurting everything out. When I was a club manager, I would say to players: "When a group of young men are away on tour, things sometimes do happen that people should keep to themselves. One of the things I always used to say to players when we were coming back was: "The tour is over – that's it". There are many things I could say after two years as England manager, but I will not be saying them myself even if I decide to write a book. Some things should stay private.'

But as Lineker observes wryly, it is difficult to imagine there can be much more to say on the subject now.

· 10 ·

Japan, and Beyond

There were all sorts of reasons why Gary Lineker decided to continue, and probably end, his career in Japan. But pre-eminent, it has to be said, was the financial inducement. It has been estimated that the former captain of England guaranteed himself the thick end of £3 million in return for signing a two-year contract with the Grampus Eight club of Nagoya. Jon Holmes cleverly deflects questions about the exact amount with talk of net and gross, but it is a fact that Tottenham's share of the package was no more than £1 million.

'It's a lot of money,' admits Holmes of Lineker's cut, 'and it will make him considerably richer if he doesn't spend too much. It is true to say the financial incentive was considerable. I don't know whether he could have got that kind of money in Europe, but it was certainly more than we had ever been offered before. I think it's fair to say we thought there might be that kind of money in it; and we asked them for more. If I'd asked them for less, I wouldn't have been doing my job.'

In other words, this is the really big financial hit after all those years of painstakingly promoting the image of Gary Lineker, goalscoring hero and every mother's favourite son, often for no monetary reward at all. If that sounds cynical, it is not meant to be; it is simply an objective assessment of a wildly successful career superbly executed and exploited by player and agent. As an object lesson in how to make the very most of a footballer's talent, in terms of both fame and fortune, this takes some beating. 'It was a good pay-off at the end of Gary's career,' agrees Jon Holmes, 'but it was a pay-off for the right reasons.'

If only Holmes, or someone like him, had been around when George Best was in his prime . . . but that, of course, is to ignore the qualities that set Lineker apart from Best, and from most other British footballers. Holmes could not have done what he has done unless Lineker had been the genuine article. The player's equability, affability and extraordinary capacity for turning the other cheek while continuing to display a real killer instinct near goal, are not an act, but the manifestation of an unusual personality. Lineker's reputation for almost saintly behaviour was as attractive to the Japanese as his internationally famous capacity for putting the ball into the opposition's net with consistent regularity. When I asked Grampus Eight why, specifically, they had recruited Lineker, the faxed answer came back: '1. He is the suitable person as the first foreign player because of his good manners in soccer games. 2. He is world famous soccer player. 3. He is highly regarded as the highest scorer. 4. Mr Hiraki, director of team, was eager to have him.'

The Englishman is just the sort of player and person the Japanese need to promote and popularise football in a country intent on becoming the first outside Europe or the Americas to stage the finals of the World Cup. 'It is a fair bet,' reported the *Daily Telegraph*'s Robert Whymant from Nagoya in November 1991 'that a year or two from now, Lineker will be a local hero. All concerned stress his 'clean' (drug-free) image, and see him as a role model.' Then Whymant went on to quote Yoshiomi Izawa, a Toyota personnel manager seconded to Grampus Eight. 'I know the English are saying we are splashing money around to get players,' observed Izawa, 'but we are not economic animals. We want someone who will fulfil young people's dreams.' Other residents of this ambitious industrial city, 150 miles west of Tokyo, see Lineker's recruitment in less idealistic terms. 'Some time soon, we'll have the (300 m.p.h.) linear bullet train and a brand new international airport. Now we are getting a world famous footballer,' an unnamed city official was quoted as saying.

Realistically, the purchase of Gary Lineker by Grampus Eight was part of a typically far-sighted and thorough Japanese masterplan to win the right to stage the finals of the 2002 World Cup and, of course, collect all the profit and prestige that goes with them. The Nagoya club are one of ten members of Japan's first fully professional league, due to be launched in May 1993. Known as the J-League, it is underpinned by the financial might of many of Japan's world-famous companies – as the decidedly exotic names of the other nine clubs may indicate. They are: Nissan Marinos, Panasonic Gamba Osaka, Mitsubishi Urawa Red Diamonds, Shimizu

S-Pulse, Yomiuri Verdy, Jef United, AS Flugels, Sanfrecce Hiroshima and Kashima Antlers. Learning from America's mistakes in trying to build a national soccer league from scratch, the Japanese have sensibly limited to three the number of foreigners each club can sign. Thus, native talent is given every opportunity to learn and develop.

Nagoya Grampus Eight, so named after a legendary mammal that is a cross between a killer whale and a dolphin and because eight is considered a lucky number by the Japanese, have the backing of 20 powerful sponsors, headed by Toyota, the second biggest motor vehicle manufacturer in the world, who own 80 per cent of the club. Nagoya, a bustling, modern, sprawling city of just over two million people, is where Toyota are based and could be described as the Detroit or Birmingham of Japan. But the gamble of promoting football in a country where Sumo wrestling, baseball, golf and even rugby are more popular sports is not wholly a matter of private enterprise. The city fathers of Nagoya, for instance, agreed to supply the £12 million needed to provide Grampus Eight with a brand new, 30,000-capacity stadium. A new training ground was also in the pipeline at the time of writing. The expectation was that the club would spend more than £4 million in setting up the training facilities and £6 million a year on players' wages and bonuses and general administration costs.

Narumi Nishigaki, managing director of Nagoya Grampus Eight Inc, has assembled a squad of 33 players, which includes two Brazilians, midfielder Jorge Putinaiti and defender Edison Rodrigues, as well as Lineker. The link between Brazilian and Japanese football is strong, as is further underlined by the re-emergence of the famous Zico from retirement to play for Kashima Antlers. He will be 40 by the time the Japanese league gets under way. Another Brazilian, Tonio, has been recruited by Shimizu S-Pulse and, of course, it was in a friendly against the Brazilian club, Corinthians, that Lineker made an introductory appearance for Grampus Eight at the start of August 1992. There is every chance, then, that the football the lone Englishman is going into, while obviously questionable in terms of overall quality, will be played with at least some guarantee of style and imagination.

Lineker certainly pronounced himself satisfied after playing for 50 minutes of the friendly against Corinthians, a 1–1 draw in which he did not score. 'I am encouraged by today's match,' he said afterwards. 'I saw a good team, some good players. I think I'll settle in.'

Needless to say, the four-day flying visit to Nagoya was conducted with all his customary charm, efficiency and flair for public relations. During that brief stay, he held two press conferences, gave seven magazine interviews and made three television appearances. At a lavish reception the night before the game, he also agreed to run from the back of the hall while the drums rolled, the spotlights flashed, the cameras clicked and most of his Grampus Eight teammates waited for him on stage. Oh yes, I almost forgot the clouds of dry ice and Hollywood-style dancing girls that helped delight the 400 guests. This is the consummate professional at work. Maybe Bobby Charlton or Bobby Moore would have done the same if they had been born 20 years later and enjoyed the expert guidance available to Lineker. But the fact remains that the lad from Leicester is the first British footballer to exploit his talent and celebrity status to an extent that is commonplace in sport on the other side of the Atlantic.

Lineker himself, of course, sees the latest chapter in his career in anything but commercial terms. 'We are really looking forward to the experience of living in a completely different culture,' he has said. 'We experienced three great years in Barcelona, but obviously this is a step further. I think the first move abroad is probably your biggest: it's perhaps the most frightening. Once you've done it and realised it can be tremendously exciting and interesting, then another move abroad is not daunting at all. In fact, it's completely the opposite. All being well, we'll enjoy the experience. Michelle, in particular, loves travelling and seeing the world. She worked on the QE2 before we got married. So she's seen quite a bit of the world already. We are really looking forward to it as regards the change of lifestyle.'

As in Barcelona, the Linekers are putting themselves out to become fluent in the language of the country currently offering Gary well-rewarded employment. During the eight-month 'sabbatical' between the end of the European Championship and leaving London for the start of the J-League season, they submitted themselves to six hours of lessons a week in Japanese, not the easiest language in the world for Europeans to learn. At the same time, the Japanese themselves have made every effort to ensure that the appropriate medical care is available for young George Lineker. Dr Yoshihisa Kodera, head of haematology at the Japanese Red Cross Hospital in Nagoya, was nominated to lead a medical team which includes a paediatrician. Grampus were even thinking of sending Dr

Kodera to London's Great Ormond Street Hospital to discuss the case history of George's leukaemia. 'All being well,' says Gary, 'checks are all that will be needed. There is no way I would do anything to jeopardise the little fellow whatsoever.'

Happily, George has responded encouragingly so far to every course of treatment. But the Linekers still face an agonising wait before knowing for certain whether their baby son has beaten the dreaded disease. 'George is doing very well,' said Gary early in 1992. 'He's done everything asked of him, and the treatment's been successful. He's got more treatment to come, but it will finish – hopefully for good – in the summer. As far as they can tell, the treatment has worked. But in all cases of leukaemia, it's whether it comes back or not. They call it a cure if he's still not got it after five years; but they say that, with his particular type of leukaemia, if it comes back, it comes back pretty quickly. I don't want to think negatively at all. We've thought positively right through, and that's what's kept us going. It's difficult to speculate on what we'd do and how we'd feel if anything went wrong.'

Despite living under that cloud, Lineker will give Grampus Eight everything that still remains of his exceptional talent for scoring goals: he knows no other way. This is no ageing superstar looking for a soft option in the twilight of his career, but a dedicated athlete determined to give value for money so long as the legs hold out. Indeed, he was at pains to point out that he was looking forward to more than just a change of lifestyle in Japan. 'I want to enjoy the football, too, and be successful,' he said. 'I don't want to go there and not play very well.'

In a sense, Lineker is going to Japan looking for some relief from the dreadful grind of English football. It is not overstating the case to say that the ever-increasing speed and competitiveness of domestic soccer helped give him an even bigger yen for the Japanese version. 'I've enjoyed my time in the English League and I've enjoyed my time at Tottenham,' he said shortly before the finals of the 1992 European Championship. 'Nothing's really changed from what I said before as regards the fact that I wanted to go out at the top; and now, I believe, is the right time. I think I probably could have stretched it to another year, but it's been a bit of a slog for everyone this season (1991–92). For the older players to match those high standards is becoming increasingly difficult. We've always played a lot of games in England, but the game has not always been played in the way it is now. It's far more physically demanding than it's ever been before, and far more teams are playing in the direct fashion that makes it very tough physically to play against.

'The major factor is that they changed the First Division/Premier League back to 22 clubs, which was an odd decision then and remains an odd decision now. A lot of players say they'd rather play than train, but I don't think that's really the issue. The problem is that we play so many games, and the character of the players is such that they will go out there and give everything they've got in every game. But the quality won't be there, because if players aren't feeling 100 per cent – which it's impossible to do if you are playing that frequently in heavy conditions – the quality will drop down and you'll get more of this stereotyped whacking it forward and trying to get rebounds. I watch the Italian stuff on television and I think, "Christ, they are quicker than us, they are sharper than us!" But they are not. It's just that they are fresher than us. That's the difference.

'The championship race has now become a case of which team can last the longest. Everybody's tired, and it just seems a shame that we went back to 22 clubs, plus all the cup competitions. The people who suffer in the end are the people who pay to watch. They are not getting the quality they deserve, and they are having to pay more for it because they are having to pay to see more football. The Premier League doesn't seem to be addressing the biggest issue of all, which is cutting down its size. The standard of football would improve for it. It's not just a question of more home games generating more money. I believe that if we played less games, we'd get better crowds and probably be able to charge more eventually because we'd be getting a better product. In a way, the direct style of play is a result of the amount of games we play. We'd all like to play the game in a nice way, but the pressure on managers to get results is such that directness is sometimes the solution.'

Lineker emphasises, though, that his criticism is directed at the structure and administration of English football, not at the players. 'I still think we've got a hell of a lot of ability in England,' he says. 'Under the circumstances, we've done tremendously well. We were great in the 1990 World Cup, for instance. I'm talking about the quality of club football more than anything else. That is suffering due to the number of games we play. The players will go through it because they are good professionals, and perhaps they don't get enough credit for what they do. They go out there, and perhaps nine of the 11 will be carrying some kind of injury; yet they carry on and give everything. But there's no zip: there's no sharpness in a lot of the games. On the Continent, they think we are crazy.

'Standards would rise if we were more sensible. All the managers agree. They all know the situation, but they are powerless to do anything about it. I know former players now say: "Oh, well. We used to play the same number of games in our day." But the game now is not quite like it was then. It is very fast, very physical. I'm not necessarily talking about hard men and getting kicked: I mean the physical demands on players. They have to get up and down the pitch all the time – particularly the wide players, the midfield players. But even the strikers are having to work harder now, because as soon as the goalkeeper gets the ball in a lot of teams, he hoofs it up the pitch. Their back-four then sprint upfield, and the striker has to bomb up to the halfway line, otherwise he's offside.

'It all takes it out of you, and I think that's the difference between the 60 games a season we played ten years ago and the 60 games a season we play now. The answer is to reduce the size of the Premier League and cut down on the number of cup competitions. You've just got to look at the product that's being offered in Italy to see the difference playing less football makes. If we, like the Italians, played only one game a week, it would be a real occasion for the fans. They would get only one home game a fortnight, and it would be something for them to look forward to. It wouldn't be a case of: 'Oh, can I afford to go and watch a game this Wednesday?' In Italy every game they play is an occasion, and they get massive support. They get it because the fans are looking forward to the game, and they can afford to spend a little bit more to get in because they haven't got to do it three times a fortnight.'

Lineker acknowledges, however, that Italian football is something of an exception, and that the problem of over-playing is not entirely confined to England. 'In Spain, they are not exactly perfect,' admits this former Barcelona player. 'They play a few midweeks, but not as many as in England. There's only one cup competition, and there are 20 teams in the top division. They extended it from 18 to 20. That's because the owners of the clubs wanted to get an extra couple of home games and the income that goes with them. That's all it is.' Sounds very familiar, doesn't it?

With his intelligence, articulateness, reputation and gift for public relations, Lineker would be a natural for high administrative office on his retirement from active participation in most other sports.

Quite clearly, too, he feels strongly enough about the unsatisfactory state of the game to want to do something about it. As he recognises, however, English football has always done its best to keep former footballers below stairs, where the establishment seem to continue to believe they belong.

'I don't deny that I wouldn't mind being involved in the game in some way when I retire, although I don't see myself as a manager,' he says. 'I would continue, hopefully, with a bit of TV work, but I want to stay around the game because I want to watch it. Football administration is a difficult area to get into, though, isn't it? Look at Bobby Charlton (who twice failed to be elected to the Football League Management Committee). If you could get administrators like that who've been through the game, know the game, it must help to improve things. Those sort of people would command more respect from the punters who watch the game and are its life-blood.

'I'm not saying I want to run football, or anything silly like that; but I would like to put something back into the game. If I could influence the game to take a step in the right direction, I'd be pleased. I don't suppose anybody will take a blind bit of notice of what I say, but who knows? You have got to try, haven't you? I mean, I'm in a position where I can get a point across because of who I am in the game. So I think it would be a shame, and a missed opportunity on my part, if I didn't express feelings that are shared by 90 per cent of English footballers. I'm gong away for a couple of years, perhaps even three, and I doubt whether I shall carry on playing when I return; but if, at some future stage, they wanted me to help English football in some way, I wouldn't close the door.'

During Lineker's brief trip to Nagoya in August 1992, the accompanying British tabloids drummed up a story about his wanting to manage England, but their headlines were more definite than the quotes underneath them – a not uncommon fault. All Lineker said, in effect, was that if the England job were to be offered to him at some future date, it would be one of the few managerial posts he would be prepared to consider taking. In other words, it was largely a diplomatic answer to a hypothetical question, and not a statement of intent.

Lineker's basic dislike of football management as a job is so intense that it would have to be a very special offer – and not just in monetary terms – to win his acceptance. 'Being a football manager is a horrible job,' he has said. 'Every player says he doesn't want to be a manager, then someone like Kevin Keegan suddenly becomes one. I'm not going to say I'll never be a manager, because it could be that, in five years' time, I might get offered the Barcelona job or something – and (tongue in cheek) I definitely wouldn't go for that! You don't know do you? If someone turns round and says here's the England job, well. . . . You can't possibly say you would never accept any job in management, but it's not something that really appeals to me at the moment.

'It's an awful job, and I couldn't stand dealing with players every day. I felt very sorry for some of the managers I've played for. It's well paid and there's a lot of good things going for them, but dealing with players – no thanks! And you are always upsetting people. All managers are hated. Every manager I've ever played for has been hated by the players. They always have to leave someone out at some stage, and that's never forgotten by players. The lads at Everton used to say this, that and the other about Howard Kendall, but he goes away and suddenly it's a case of: "Christ, it's not like it was under Howard!" Then he comes back, and it's not like it used to be under the previous manager. The grass is always greener on the other side so far as players are concerned.'

Jon Holmes feels his client's talents could be used best to strike a healthier balance between supply and demand in English football. 'Gary knows a lot about marketing the game,' he says, 'and that's what English football should really be into. That means not just pulling the cheap profit, but seeing the long-term future. Gary himself has never taken any decisions in football just for money, but we've done all right financially. I believe that's the right way to do it. You don't just chase the money, you think about what you are actually trying to achieve. And if the quality's good enough, then the money follows on. The problem is that too many people find short-term routes. Just following money decisions in the game – like adding extra competitions – can't be right. I think players having a say in the game is more important than the share-out of the TV money. It's interesting that the games that are run by ex-players, like tennis and golf, have actually grown more in the past few years. You could argue a bit about tennis, but not about golf. It has been marketed brilliantly.'

As to the marketing of Gary Lineker in Japan, Holmes takes the all-round, long-term view as usual. 'Moneywise, it is an attractive package and it has a lot of elements in it that work. The idea of doing pioneering work in Japanese football appealed to Gary, and you are also associated with a very strong company like Toyota.

There are long-term possibilities there, and he's got to think about what he's going to do beyond Grampus Eight.' But does not this extremely lucrative deal mean that the Linekers do not have to worry about money from now on? 'There's a lot of talk in football about people having enough money to last them the rest of their lives,' he adds, 'but it depends at what standard you live. If you are used to living on a salary of £200,000 a year, say, you've got to amass a lot of money to be able to continue to live on £200,000 once that salary stops.' In other words, watch this space.

Gary Lineker – Career Record

631 first-class matches (322 goals), including 80 internationals (48 goals) and 439 League games (236 goals). Figures also include one B appearance for England.

League games: Leicester City 194 (95 goals), Everton 41 (30 goals), Barcelona 99 (44 goals), Tottenham Hotspur 105 (67 goals).

Football Writers Association player of the year 1986, 1992.

Professional Footballers Association player of the year 1986.

Transfer fees: Leicester to Everton £800,000; Everton to Barcelona £2,200,000; Barcelona to Tottenham £1,100,000; Tottenham to Grampus Eight £1,000,000.

Top scorer World Cup 1986 with six goals.

FIFA Fair Play Prize 1990 for never being booked or sent off.

1988 Spanish Cup winners medal; 1989 European Cup-Winners' Cup winners medal; 1991 FA Cup winners medal.

Awarded OBE New Year's Honours List 1992.

International Appearances

Dates	Venue	Opponents	Result	Goals
1983–84:				
1984 26 May	Hampden Park	Scotland	1–1	
1984–85:				
1985 26 March	Wembley	Republic of Ireland	2–1	1
1985 1 May	Bucharest	Romania	0–0	
1985 25 May	Hampden Park	Scotland	0–1	
1985 6 June	Mexico City	Italy	1–2	
1985 12 June	Mexico City	West Germany	3–0	
1985 16 June	Los Angeles	USA	5–0	2
1985–86:				
1985 11 September	Wembley	Romania	1–1	
1985 16 October	Wembley	Turkey	5–0	3
1985 13 November	Wembley	Northern Ireland	0–0	
1986 29 January	Cairo	Egypt	4–0	
1986 26 March	Tbilisi	USSR	1–0	

Dates	Venue	Opponents	Result	Goals
1986 24 May	Vancouver	Canada	1–0	
1986 3 June	Monterrey	Portugal	0–1	
1986 6 June	Monterrey	Morocco	0–0	
1986 11 June	Poland	Poland	3–0	3
1986 18 June	Mexico City	Paraguay	3–0	2
1986 22 June	Mexico City	Argentina	1–2	1
1986–87:				
1986 15 October	Wembley	Northern Ireland	3–0	2
1986 12 November	Wembley	Yugoslavia	2–0	
1987 18 February	Madrid	Spain	4–2	4
1987 1 April	Belfast	Northern Ireland	2–0	
1987 29 April	Izmir	Turkey	0–0	
1987 19 May	Wembley	Brazil	1–1	1
1987–88:				
1987 9 September	Dusseldorf	West Germany	1–3	1
1987 14 October	Wembley	Turkey	8–0	3
1987 11 November	Belgrade	Yugoslavia	4–1	
1988 23 March	Wembley	Holland	2–2	1
1988 27 April	Budapest	Hungary	0–0	
1988 21 May	Wembley	Scotland	1–0	
1988 24 May	Wembley	Colombia	1–1	1
1988 28 May	Lausanne	Switzerland	1–0	1
1988 12 June	Stuttgart	Republic of Ireland	0–1	
1988 15 June	Dusseldorf	Holland	1–3	
1988 18 June	Frankfurt	USSR	1–3	
1988–89:				
1988 19 October	Wembley	Sweden	0–0	
1988 16 November	Riyadh	Saudi Arabia	1–1	
1989 8 February	Athens	Greece	2–1	
1989 8 March	Tirana	Albania	2–0	
1989 26 April	Wembley	Albania	5–0	1
1989 3 June	Wembley	Poland	3–0	1
1989 7 June	Copenhagen	Denmark	1–1	1
1989–90:				
1989 6 September	Stockholm	Sweden	0–0	
1989 11 October	Katowice	Poland	0–0	
1989 15 November	Wembley	Italy	0–0	
1989 13 December	Wembley	Yugoslavia	2–1	
1990 28 March	Wembley	Brazil	1–0	1
1990 25 April	Wembley	Czechoslovakia	4–2	
1990 15 May	Wembley	Denmark	1–0	1
1990 22 May	Wembley	Uruguay	1–2	
1990 6 June	Tunis	Tunisia	1–1	
1990 11 June	Cagliari	Republic of Ireland	1–1	1
1990 16 June	Cagliari	Holland	0–0	
1990 21 June	Cagliari	Egypt	1–0	
1990 26 June	Bologna	Belgium	1–0	
1990 1 July	Naples	Cameroon	3–2	2 (2 pens)

Dates	Venue	Opponents	Result	Goals
1990 4 July	Turin	West Germany	1–1	1
1990 7 July	Bari	Italy	1–2	
1990–1991:				
1990 12 September	Wembley	Hungary	1–0	1
1990 17 October	Wembley	Poland	2–0	1 (pen)
1990 14 November	Dublin	Republic of Ireland	1–1	
1991 6 February	Wembley	Cameroon	2–0	2 (1 pen)
1991 27 March	Wembley	Republic of Ireland	1–1	
1991 1 May	Izmir	Turkey	1–0	
1991 25 May	Wembley	Argentina	2–2	1
1991 1 June	Sydney	Australia	1–0	
1991 3 June	Auckland	New Zealand	1–0	1
1991 12 June	Kuala Lumpur	Malaysia	4–2	4
1991–92:				
1991 11 September	Wembley	Germany	0–1	
1991 16 October	Wembley	Turkey	1–0	
1991 13 November	Poznan	Poland	1–1	1
1992 19 February	Wembley	France	2–0	1
1992 25 March	Prague	Czechoslovakia	2–2	
1992 29 April	Moscow	CIS	2–2	1
1992 12 May	Budapest	Hungary	1–0	
1992 17 May	Wembley	Brazil	1–1	
1992 3 June	Helsinki	Finland	2–1	
1992 11 June	Malmo	Denmark	0–0	
1992 14 June	Malmo	France	0–0	
1992 17 June	Stockholm	Sweden	1–2	

England's Top Ten Post-War Goalscorers
(Figures in brackets denote number of matches)

1	Bobby Charlton	49	(106)
2	Gary Lineker	48	(80)
3	Jimmy Greaves	44	(57)
4	Nat Lofthouse	30	(33)
5	Tom Finney	30	(76)
6	Bryan Robson	26	(89)
7	Geoff Hurst	24	(49)
8	Stan Mortensen	23	(25)
9	Mike Channon	21	(46)
10	Kevin Keegan	21	(63)

Index